THE TSIMSHIAN INDIANS AND THEIR ARTS

THE TSIMSHIAN INDIANS

AND THEIR ARTS

THE TSIMSHIAN AND THEIR NEIGHBORS

By Viola E. Garfield

TSIMSHIAN SCULPTURE

By Paul S. Wingert

UNIVERSITY OF WASHINGTON PRESS

Seattle and London

Originally published as Parts 1 and 2 of
The Tsimshian: Their Arts and Music,
Publication XVIII of the American Ethnological Society,
edited by Marian W. Smith

Printed in the United States of America

To the Memories of

FRANZ BOAS

AND

HEINRICH WILHELM AUGUSTIN

TABLE OF CONTENTS

List of Illustrations

PLATES

Plate 1, a. Bryan Peel, the Nass River carver, using the drill. Note the tool box and two finished rattles.

b. Using the straight knife on the upper half of a rattle. The lower half lies on the work block.

c. Using the adz to shape the lower half of a rattle.

PART 1

Viola E. Garfield

THE TSIMSHIAN AND THEIR NEIGHBORS

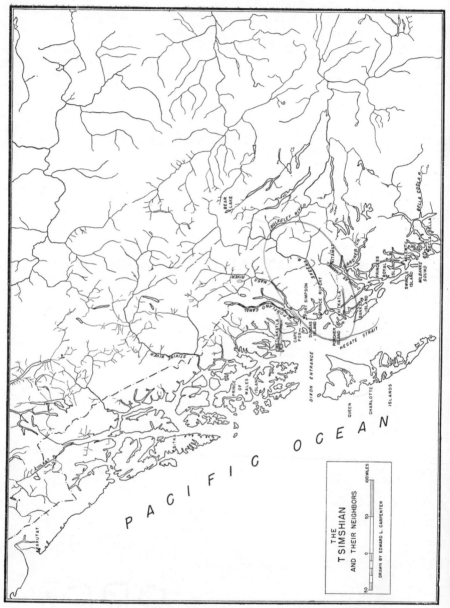

Figure 1

PREFACE

My first view of the Tsimshian was of rows of houses spaced along the meandering shores of New Metlakatla, Alaska. Approaching the island in a late August afternoon Purple Mountain and Yellow Hill with their brilliant colors dwarfed the weathered homes and churches. Six school teachers and the superintendent were arriving to spend the winter in an Indian village. The arrival of the teachers was an annual event for which the villagers were well prepared by long experience. Only two of us had ever met Indians before and none of us had known such people as the Metlakatlans. In the balance sheet of that winter, they fared better than we and the next fall saw another six arriving to take our vacated places.

Many adult Metlakatlans had helped build the town and all but the youngest had known its founder. They were people who had chosen to leave their homeland, not only to settle in the wilderness in a new country, but who had vowed to renounce the customs of their forefathers. They had the reputation of being the most progressive of all Northwest Coast Indian tribes, meaning that they best approximated the way of life of the Whites who thus evaluated them. Yet in many ways the Metlakatlans displayed attitudes, beliefs and behavior that were foreign and incomprehensible to the teachers.

My own curiosity and interest lay dormant for several years before there was an opportunity to learn something of the cultural heritage that motivated the Metlakatlans. The quest for an understanding of their background led to Port Simpson, British Columbia, where relatives of the majority of Metlakatlans now reside, and thence to the borders of Tsimshian territory in northern British Columbia and, beyond, to surrounding native peoples.

Most of the literature on the Tsimshian pertains to the villages of the lower Skeena River and coast, and much of our knowledge of them has been extracted from myths and tales. There are brief papers on Coast Tsimshian and Nisqa social organization but next to nothing on Nisqa material culture, economy or political structure. Before the maritime fur trade drew the Nisqa down the river to the coast there must have been significant differences between the tribesmen of the lower river and those who roamed the mountainous regions bordering the upper Nass. There is almost nothing in the literature about the Kitkatlas, the most southerly tribe. The Port Simpson people regard them as the most conservative of all Tsimshian groups who preserve the rank and prestige system and

3

many elements of potlatching, hereditary chieftainship and contractual marriage.

The principal literature on the Gitksan describes clan and lineage legends illustrated on totem-pole carvings. These legends give evidence of intimate contact with Athapascans and extensive borrowing from them. Many Gitksan families trace ancestors and crest possessions to wild rice gatherers and bulb eaters of the interior plateaus and lakes rather than to river and sea fishermen.

Three elements of Tsimshian culture set them off most distinctly from their neighbors. The language is distinct and, to date, no relationship between it and any others in the area has been demonstrated. The Tsimshian have four exogamous kinship divisions in contrast to the dual divisions of the Tlingit and Haida, though all four phratries are not represented in every Tsimshian town. The Coast Tsimshian and Nisqa elevated certain lineage heads to tribal chiefs whose prestige was greatly enhanced by tribal economic support and, properties, and by tribute from all members of the local group regardless of clan affiliation. They did not take the further step of delegating the power of law enforcement to tribal chiefs.

In the following presentation of the main features of Tsimshian culture, it is apparent that we lack descriptive information for the northern Gitksan particularly, and that we lack much comparative data on relationships between the Tsimshian and their neighbors. There is also little historical depth to our data. Some of these gaps can be filled by comparative analytical studies of the Tsimshian with other tribes of Northwest America, using existing literary sources. Other problems will only be solved in the future by systematic field work.

September, 1950   Viola E. Garfield
Seattle, Washington

CHAPTER ONE

THE TSIMSHIAN AND THEIR NEIGHBORS

The Tsimshian lived along the banks and tributaries of the Nass and Skeena Rivers in British Columbia. They ranged the lakes and plateaus between the two streams, and to Portland Canal northwest of the Nass. The sea coast and coastal islands between the estuaries of the Nass and Skeena belonged to them and they also explored and settled on some of the islands, the most southerly of which was Swindle Island, south of Princess Royal Island (see Fig. 1). South of Skeena River the salt water inlets and streams flowing into them belonged mainly to the northern Kwakiutl-speaking Xaihais (Heiltsuq) and Xaisla (Kitimat). Further south were the Bella Bella and the Salishan-speaking Bella Coola. There were Tsimshian villages and camps on lower Douglas Channel where the territory of the Kitimat and Tsimshian joined, and on some of the islands. The Kitqa'ata in Hartley Bay and Nepean Sound, and the Kitkiata above them on Douglas Channel are practically extinct. The Kitasu on Laredo Channel near the southeast end of Princess Royal Island are no longer a separate tribe of Tsimshian.

The Haida on Queen Charlotte and Prince of Wales Islands were the western neighbors of the Tsimshian, and the Tlingit were their north-western neighbors beyond Dixon Entrance and Portland Canal. Inland were Athapascan-speaking peoples.

The Tsimshian were a culturally and linguistically cohesive group whose habitat included the sea coast, coastal islands and river basins on both sides of the coast range, and who therefore were adapted to varied ecological conditions. The habitat of most northern Northwest Coast tribes was the western or seaward side of the coast range and permanent villages were on tidewater. In Washington, Oregon and northern California a coastal plain separates the mountains from the sea. Southern coastal peoples either dwelt along rivers and seldom descended to salt water or they lived on tidewater and went inland only to trade or hunt. In contrast to these peoples, the Tsimshian were mountain as well as sea dwellers.

North of the Gulf of Georgia, the submerged mountains form a coast broken by bays and long, narrow inlets. It is sheltered from the ocean by numerous islands. Heavy rainfall on the seaward side of the mountains feeds numerous lakes and streams which abound in fish, especially salmon and olachen. There is little snowfall, and temperatures are

5

moderate throughout the year, lacking the extremes prevalent in the interior. The land is heavily forested with red and yellow cedar, spruce, fir and hemlock. Marshes covered with deep layers of wet, spongy mosses, called muskeg, render flat areas impassable much of the year. The rocky, precipitous topography, heavy timber, jungle-like ground cover of devil's club and other shrubbery, and areas of muskeg make land travel and hunting difficult in the coastal area. The drier, more open country north and east of the coast range is much more favorable for hunting and land transportation. There are no dense forests. Local stands of alder, maple, willow, yew, black pine, spruce and birch prevail, but there are few of the cedars utilized so effectively by the coastal people, except in the valleys of the Nass and Skeena Rivers.

The Nass, navigable by canoe for about eighty miles, and the Skeena navigable to Qaldo two hundred and fifty miles inland, provided the Tsimshian with access to the ocean and the inter-mountain plateaus. A number of inlets, particularly Portland Canal and Douglas Channel allowed exploitation of a protected sea coast as well as the hinterland.

The Tsimshian language was once classified as Penutian by the late Dr. Edward Sapir, but without substantiating evidence. Dr. Harry Hoijer classifies it as a separate stock.[1] It is spoken in three main, mutually intelligible dialects: Nisqa on the Nass River; Gitksan on the upper Skeena and its tributaries; and Tsimshian proper or Coast Tsimshian on the lower Skeena, Douglas Channel and the islands. South of the Skeena estuary the Kitkatla on Porcher, Dolphin and McCauley Islands speak a dialect which is a variant of Coast Tsimshian. Cultural differences also distinguish the Nisqa, Gitksan and Coast Tsimshian; those of the south show greater cultural affiliations with their Kwakiutl neighbors and those above the canyon of the Skeena were influenced by inland Athapascan cultures.

In a consideration of the Tsimshian and their place in the Northwest Coast area, language is a factor of prime importance. Linguists have not been able to relate the Tsimshian language specifically to any other, either of North America or Asia. Tsimshian lacks functional tone which is characteristic of all neighboring Nadene speakers, excepting Haida. In this general sense, it resembles the Salish languages to the south. The phonetic patterns of all coastal languages from northern California to, but not including, the Eskimo share many similarities and point either to remotely related dialects or to a long period of slow diffusion and borrowing. Investigations so far made do not permit us to decide whether there are also fundamental grammatical concepts that are similar. While it seems highly probable that Tsimshian is distantly related to other languages of the North Pacific, it is modernly so distinct

---

[1] Hoijer, 1946, p. 15.

as to defy classification. Whatever its affiliations prove to be, Tsimshian as now known developed over a period of several hundred years in the area bounded by the Nass and Skeena Rivers, and it cannot be considered as a recent phenomenon.

Early Contacts with Europeans

The explorations and maritime fur trade of the last quarter of the eighteenth century did not touch the Tsimshian as directly as they did the Tlingit and Haida. However, the demand for pelts was undoubtedly a factor which accelerated movement of Nass and Skeena River people to the coast where they were able to participate in the catch and the foreign trade goods.

Continental explorers and fur traders did not reach any part of Tsimshian country until about 1830, though iron and other trade goods must have filtered through to them long before that date. By the first decade of the nineteenth century maritime furs were scarce and rivalry between the Russian American Company and the Hudson's Bay Company for control of what is now western Canada and adjacent Alaska was reaching a crisis.

The first Hudson's Bay fort west of the Rockies was built in 1805 on the north end of McLeod Lake. It was too far east to reach the Tsimshian. Fort Connelly on Bear Lake at the head of a branch of the Skeena was established in 1826. This was near the northernmost Gitksan. Fort Simpson was built at the mouth of the Nass River in 1831 and moved to Tsimshian Peninsula, about twenty miles north of Prince Rupert, in 1834. The latter site was the camping ground of the Tsimshian from Metlakatla on their way to and from the Nass. They dismantled their homes and rebuilt them on either side of the post. By 1857, 2,300 Indians lived in or near the village, including most of the residents of former lower Skeena River towns and Metlakatla and many southern Tsimshian.

Fort Simpson attracted other Indians, especially the Haida who came by the hundreds with their canoes, potatoes, fish and furs to trade with the Tsimshian as well as with the English.

In 1836, the Hudson's Bay Company built a post at the north end of Lake Babine. Coastal Tsimshian had a regular trading route to Bulkeley canyon, where the river joins the Skeena, and a monopoly of trade with the Babines. The coastal people brought trade goods from Fort Simpson and preserved sea foods which they bartered to the Babines for furs. It was probably as early as 1836 that Legeax, a tribal chief at Fort Simpson, undertook to monopolize Skeena River trade with the coast, a monopoly which he maintained until about 1868. The role of the Gitksan in this trade is not clear. They seem to have submitted to Coast Tsimshian entering their territory for direct trade with the Babines and, in fact, to have bartered their furs for goods from the coast.[2]

The main influence of the Hudson's Bay Company on the Tsimshian was through control of prices and wages, and was therefore economic. A few Indians were trained to read and write, to act as interpreters and serve in minor capacities on boats and in industries. A few women were taken into the forts as menials and fewer still as wives. There were no schools or missions, a situation which factors deplored.

A turning point in the lives of many Fort Simpson natives came in 1857 with the arrival of twenty-one year old William Duncan, sent by the Church Missionary Society of London to christianize and educate the Tsimshian.[3] He laid the foundation for his work by learning the Tsimshian language and something of their customs, then started a school and church in the village. It soon became apparent to him that the success of his venture was imperiled by conditions at the Fort. In 1862, he led a party of fifty back to the salt-water channels, abandoned when the post was built. There they built a new village which they named Metlakatla.

Mr. Duncan organized a cooperative store and purchased a schooner to provide villagers with trade goods at reasonable prices and as a direct outlet for their furs to Victoria. A sawmill and boat-building plant provided them with lumber for homes and public buildings and with canoes and river boats for freighting and trading. Provisions were made for the election of men to serve as councilmen, policemen, firemen and church elders, subject to Mr. Duncan's approval. Musical talents of the Tsimshian found outlet in the church choir and in learning to play the organ and band instruments donated to them in 1870. Photographic equipment and a printing press recorded the progress of the town and its people.

Controversies between Mr. Duncan and the Bishop representing the Church Missionary Society led to his dismissal in 1881. As the Church claimed the property on which the town was built, Mr. Duncan had no alternative than to leave. He visited Washington, D. C., and received assurance that he would be welcome to establish a colony in Alaska. Accordingly, eight hundred and twenty-five of the nine hundred and fifty inhabitants emigrated from Metlakatla to Port Chester on Annette Island, seventeen miles from Ketchikan, and began the construction of a new town in August, 1887. By act of Congress in 1891, the island was set aside for them and any other Indians who wished to join them, the only Indian reservation so designated in Alaska to the present time.

The pattern of the old colony was repeated in New Metlakatla under Mr. Duncan's direction until 1914 when the Office of Indian Affairs took

[2] Dee, 1944—45. Work's journal contains many references to the Coast Tsimshian then living a few miles south of the post enclosure.
[3] Arctander, 1909.

over management of the school and health services. At Mr. Duncan's death in 1918, his private fortune was left in trust to the village. These funds, administered by the town council, have given the people of New Metlakatla more freedom than is enjoyed by any other native group in Alaska or in British Columbia.

Mr. Duncan made his first mission trip to the Nass in 1860, visiting all the principal villages. A mission was built at Kuinwoch in 1864 and moved to Kincolith in 1867. A Methodist mission was also established on the river in 1874. Though the men in charge initiated many changes in the customs and standard of living of the Nisqa none of them had the long tenure and the business acumen of Mr. Duncan. Also, the Nisqa lived in a region that was not strategically located either during the fur trade era nor the more recent ones of gold rushes and colonization; their river was not a navigable route into the interior and their villages were periodically undermined by floods.

The first mission within reach of the Gitksan was established at Fort Babine in 1847. Lay workers from Metlakatla also visited the Gitksan. The Western Union Telegraph line went through Gitksan territory in 1865—67 and furnished them employment and, when it was abandoned, with wire and equipment which they utilized. Discovery of gold at Barkersville in 1867 brought white men, their wares and ways into the area, and the building of the railroad from Prince Rupert to Hazelton along the Skeena brought them into further contact. On the whole, the Gitksan have been less influenced by outsiders than their Nisqa and Coast Tsimshian relatives. There are few white settlers in the area between the Nass and the Skeena.

A comparative study of the towns of New Metlakatla and Port Simpson would be rewarding. Families now at Port Simpson are mainly descendants of those who refused to join Mr. Duncan's colony of Old Metlakatla. Those now living in New Metlakatla are descendants of a doubly screened group; first in the move to Old Metlakatla and then to Alaska. Almost the whole Gitlan tribe followed their leader from Fort Simpson to Old Metlakatla, while the Gispaxloats chief kept the greater number of his followers at the Fort. For a number of years, Legeax, the Gispaxloats chief, was the leader in a revival of old customs. At the present time, the Port Simpson people observe many more of the ways of their forefathers than do the people of New Metlakatla.

Settlements

Winter villages of the Tsimshian were located on the banks of streams or alongside salt-water beaches. About twenty-five settlements are known from the nineteenth century. Those located on fresh water were on the banks of the Nass and Skeena except Kitwinkool on the river by the same name, a tributary of the Skeena. Kitwinkool was on the Grease Trail between Kitwanga on the Skeena and Gitlaxdamks on the Nass, a trade route over which olachen oil from the Nass estuary reached the interior.

Since travel on the rivers and coast was mainly by canoe, a house or village site was chosen where craft could be readily landed and beached. A level, well-drained location was also necessary since houses had only earth or sand floors. Houses always faced a beach or stream and were arranged in a single row if space permitted. Additional rows stood back of the first, separated by paths. The first row stood as near the water as possible to facilitate loading and unloading canoes. Another factor in selection of a site was the ease with which it could be protected from raiders. The Tsimshian preferred a point of land that commanded a view of water approaches, or was backed by woods and swamp that would retard or discourage enemies. Most sites were unsuited to modern conditions of travel, and only a few are still occupied. Permanent villages probably averaged less than a hundred people. A settlement of maximal size had no more than five hundred. However, as many as two thousand congregated at the Nass olachen fishing grounds or at the larger trading centers for periods of several weeks.

Cedar trees grew throughout the Nass and Skeena River valleys, providing the Tsimshian with planks for homes and furnishings, and logs for canoes. In most of the area of western British Columbia and southeastern Alaska there is a dry belt back of the coast range which limits the size and variety of trees. Straight grained spruce, which grows in the interior, can be split but is not as workable nor as durable as cedar. Unlike their inland Athapascan neighbors who built homes of poles and small logs, the Tsimshian constructed the coast type of low gabled plank house throughout their whole area.

Tsimshian homes were rectangular plank houses of moderate size.[4] There were no structures used exclusively for community social or religious functions. The Tsimshian occasionally built girls' puberty huts, though adolescents were more frequently confined in an enclosure within the house. They did not use the sweat lodges or elevated caches which were customary to their Athapascan neighbors.

Most Tsimshian houses had flat earth or sand floors though a few had excavated interiors. In either case, the family cooking fires were in the center, surrounded by firewood, smooth stones for food boiling, wooden tongs, cooking boxes and serving dishes. A platform along the walls served as beds, seats and storage space for family possessions. Food was stored in boxes in the cool earth underneath. Goods were kept in large carved or painted wooden chests. Most of the dried foods were stored on

[4] Boas, 1916, pp. 46—49. Drawings of the house plan and framework are included.

shelves suspended from the beams and rafters, or hung in bundles from the beams. Here they were safe from damage and were kept dry by heat from the fire. In some houses a narrow space to the back was set apart by a half-partition. This was a storage room where dancing paraphernalia and crest ornaments were stored. Initiates emerged from it or property was brought out during potlatches. The space at the back of the house was reserved for the house head, his family and possessions. On either side, compartments were assigned to nephews, brothers or other close male relatives and their families. Slaves with their few possessions lived in the coldest section of the house on either side of the door. The houses of chiefs were generally larger than other homes because chiefs entertained more and their dwellings were used for public gatherings.

When the Whites came into the area new ideas and styles in house interiors developed. The first innovations were windows in the front walls and hinged doors that replaced the skin or board covers of earlier days. Windows took the place of facade paintings as symbols of prestige and affluence. The second stage of innovation was the building of houses of milled lumber either with or without wooden floors. The next change in fashion introduced homes which externally resembled those of the western pioneers who had brought architectural ideas from England or eastern Canada. The interior floor plan was also modified by some builders to include one large, high-ceilinged room as a family gathering place and several very small rooms as sleeping and storage spaces. A few houses were built without any interior partitions. Such houses have lately given way to modern bungalows indistinguishable from those built in the last thirty years in any small town in Canada or the United States. No examples of the plank type of community house survive and none has been lived in since about 1900.

Tsimshian families also built smokehouses and camp cabins at each fishing and hunting site. Both structures were similar to the permanent homes, though usually more roughly built. Many families had well-built cabins at fish camps which were visited every year; other families lived in temporary lean-to or gabled shelters, or in smokehouses. These were sometimes covered with bark or mats instead of planks. Preserved foods were stored in cabins or smokehouses until the family returned to the winter town or until needed.

Fortifications have been described for many of the tribes of the Northwest Coast. Details on Tsimshian forts are meager. They were built on hills or rocky promontories and were equipped with shelters and provisions. A double fence of logs and a heavy door which could be let down on enemies are also described. Logs and rocks were fastened about the base of the walls to be released on invading enemies. Fortified villages are briefly described in both Coast Tsimshian and Gitksan folktales.

Transportation

Canoes were essential to Tsimshian life on the Nass and Skeena Rivers, and especially so on the coast. The large cedar trees of the coastal area furnished material for canoes capable of long voyages and of carrying whole families and as much as three tons of freight. Economic exploitation of extensive areas and the accumulation of bulky, heavy household goods were facilitated by the size, boyancy and maneuverability of canoes. One of the properties of cedar is that it can be bent or stretched by the application of moisture and heat. When the adzing of a canoe was nearly complete, it was filled with water which was heated by adding hot stones. When the wood was sufficiently softened thwarts were forced into the sides gradually stretching the log to the desired width. The greatest width of a finished canoe was about one and one-half times the diameter of the log. Thus Northwest canoes were much more stable and seaworthy than they would have been had the makers used the unstretched log.

Marine architects today consider the Northwest canoe excellent and seaworthy in design. Its only defect lay in its tendency to split when subjected to heavy quartering seas. Haida tales dwell on the dangers of drowning from such a mishap. The Haida islands were much more exposed to such dangers than were most Tsimshian districts where protection could be found behind some sheltering island, or where customary routes did not extend across open sea. The Tsimshian acquired their finest canoes from the Haida, who were renowned for the size and excellence of their craft.

In the late nineteenth century, canoes were replaced by sail boats of European design, either manufactured by the natives or purchased from White traders. Of late years gasboats have in turn replaced sailing craft. Gasboats are quite as essential to families living in isolated Northwest Coast towns as automobiles are to dwellers on rural roads and highways.

The Tsimshian living or traveling on the lakes and streams of the interior used small dugout or bark canoes, or built rafts for temporary use. A light weight canoe was desirable where frequent portages must be negotiated or where a combination of land and water travel was necessary to reach a destination. Canoes used in the interior were not constructed with the skill and care that were lavished on the huge cedar log craft of the large rivers and coast. However, they are still used to some extent for local travel where gasboats cannot navigate and motors are too cumbersome to carry.

Snowshoes were worn for winter travel on the high plateaus back of the coast range. The Coastal Tsimshian, Tlingit and Haida of Prince of Wales Island occasionally wore them for fall and winter hunting and trapping but they did not lend themselves to travel on the rocky terrain and jungle-like growth along the coast. Tsimshian snowshoes were similar to those of their Athapascan neighbors.[5]

Athapascans packed loads on dogs, but no information on this method of lightening the load for human beings is available for the Tsimshian living in the interior. The Coast Tsimshian did not use dog packs.

Foods and Ownership of Resources

Salmon was the decisive food resource of the Tsimshian, as it was of most other Northwest Coast tribes. Cohoes or spring salmon and sockeye salmon furnished the bulk of fish dried for winter use, though humpback salmon were also stored in quantity. Humpbacks were available almost anywhere on the coast and islands after the other runs were over, even as late as November. Some salmon could be caught during the winter to relieve the monotony of smoked dried fish.

Olachen, a variety of candlefish with high oil content, was second in importance among the basic seafood resources. The largest runs of olachen occurred in the Nass River beginning in late February or early March and continuing occasionally as late as May. Olachen was especially welcome because it came early in the spring when stores of dried food were apt to be low, and fresh food was scarce. All the Tsimshian looked forward to olachen fishing at the mouth of the Nass, where they were joined by Haida and Tlingit fishermen and traders. Olachen spawned in many other streams along the coast as far north as Copper River, though none came in to the Queen Charlotte Islands. The vast numbers which congregated in the estuary of the Nass made that district a center of the oil making industry. Herring were also caught and dried or rendered into oil. Deep sea fishing for cod and halibut off Dundas, Porcher and Banks Islands was another important activity of the Coast Tsimshian. Hair seals and sea lions were hunted on these islands as well as on more protected islands, and seals were also taken along the lower courses of the Nass and Skeena Rivers. Bear and deer hunting on the islands and mainland, and mountain-goat hunting on the mainland, furnished both food and skins. Berries grow in many varieties and great profusion in most of the Tsimshian territory. Shellfish and seaweed, collected by the women, were important barter and food items.

Almost everything edible in the area was utilized. Minor resources such as shoots, roots, crabapples, barnacles, chitons and barks added variety to the fish, meat and berry diet. The Tsimshian were able to take advantage of the perishable, seasonal abundance of foods because of their knowledge of efficient techniques of drying and smoking fish, meat and berries, rending oil from fish and seals, and preserving meat and

[5] Davidson, 1937, p. 184. Two-piece frame, hexagonal weave, turned up toe or flat, wrapped fastening, toe hole.

berries by sealing them in fat. Ordinarily the coastal area was too damp for sun and wind drying, so smokehouses were constructed or racks were used over slow fires out-of-doors.

It was characteristic of the Tsimshian, as of other Northwest Coast tribes that exclusive rights to exploit resource districts were claimed by kin. Lineages of the Tsimshian were the owners of rights to hunt, fish, pick berries or gather raw materials from geographically defined territories. Lineage properties were listed at an installation potlatch of a new head, hence were in his name. Lineage heads could, and did, designate certain areas as exclusive and pass them on as private property to successors. Lineage heads also acquired exclusive rights by gift, as compensation for murder of a relative or other wrong, by occupying and using unclaimed territory, by discovery and by seizure. Tribal chiefs acquired exclusive rights by the same means as lineage heads.

In theory, rights to territories, properly validated in potlatches and established by use and occupancy, were inalienable. Actually, there is ample evidence that these rights did change hands even before the Whites arrived to disrupt former patterns. Rights extended as a temporary courtesy to newcomers sometimes became permanent through occupation. Failure to use an area was regarded as abandonment and the district was opened to new claimants. Abandonment probably occurred more frequently in the nineteenth century than previously due to decimation of native populations and increased participation in new economic pursuits introduced by the Whites.

In pre-European times new camps and towns were established on unoccupied, unclaimed or seized sites. The original single family or two roamed the countryside and appropriated whatever they needed. As additional families joined them adjacent and accessible areas were divided among the various lineages, not always peaceably, until all of the productive lands and shores were apportioned. Lineage-owned districts extended along the rivers and shores, and back into the hinterland wherever there were foods or raw materials and means of access. Though it is difficult to document, it is probable that the boundaries of owned areas were not sharply defined in heavily wooded, mountainous country which could not be easily reached from streams or the shores of inlets and lakes. There is also no information on whether or not any difference in attitude existed toward trespass upon areas from which staple foods were taken yearly, and upon those from which supplies were taken only occasionally or in negligible quantity and value.

By the time Europeans arrived, there were no unclaimed land or sea food resources of a kind important in the Indians' economy. Though no directly comparable data are available for the Tsimshian, this fact is strikingly shown in surveys made in 1945 in connection with United States government hearings on Tlingit and Haida claims in southeastern

Alaska.[6] Not only were lands and beaches listed by the Indians as lineage property, but also offshore cod and halibut banks, and seal and sea-lion rocks. But for much of the rugged inland the evidence presented by witnesses did not substantiate claims of regular or intensive use. Trapping by a few men, sporadic hunting, and an occasional exploratory trip constituted the use made of inland areas not easily accessible from the shores of inlets or banks of navigable streams. The white man in Alaska has followed the same pattern as the Indian, for he has made no use whatever of much of the inland areas, and only specialized or casual use of others for mining, timber cutting or hunting.

Organization for Production

Organization for the collection and conversion of foods and raw materials was in the hands of lineage and tribal heads. They planned seasonal movements of their own groups, though there was a strong tendency for the winter village to break up into individual family units, particularly for salmon fishing. Chiefs delegated work to their immediate relatives, wives, children and slaves and set a goal of the quantities to be collected. They supervised men's work while their senior wives supervised the labor of younger women and female slaves. Feasts, potlatches and major undertakings like the building of a new house, were planned several years in advance and surpluses were accumulated in accordance with such long range plans.

The seasonal runs of salmon, herring and olachen set the pattern for the yearly cycle of economic activities. Hordes of fish milled about the estuaries or fought their way along the streams to spawning grounds and attracted native fishermen as they do commercial fishermen today. Spring and summer were busy seasons when food was preserved and stored for the stormy months from November through February. Since most of the entertaining and feasting took place during the winter, each family had to store sufficient provisions to meet the demands of trading, feasting, potlatching, purchase of services and payment of debts in addition to its daily needs.

For all of those within reach of the olachen runs on the coastal rivers, the year began in February or March. Salmon runs began in May or early June and extended through October. Berry picking and collection of materials for household furnishings, implements, clothing and dwellings were also made during the summer months. Women gathered berries, vegetable foods and shellfish as well as grasses, roots and bark for weaving. Offshore fishing occupied the attention of at least some of the men. Seal and sea-lion hunting were done throughout most of the year

[6] Goldschmidt and Haas, 1946.

though the main supplies were taken during the spring and summer. Fall hunting ended the seasonal activities for most families.

The tribal chief in each village decided when his group should move to the olachen fishing grounds and led the exodus with the members of his household and those of his nearest relatives and leading lineage heads. After the olachen fishing was over families scattered to salmon streams belonging to lineages of the men and there seems to have been little tribal control during the rest of the food-gathering season. Lineage heads directed operations and tribal chiefs moved to their own fish camps with retinues of relatives, retainers and slaves. There were always heads of lineages of a chief's own clan who stayed with him and there were also men without resource districts or close relatives who attached themselves to the tribal chiefs.

There was some specialization in production, both village and individual. The Nisqa and Coast Tsimshian from Metlakatla produced most of the olachen oil. The Nisqa bartered their surpluses across the Grease Trail to the interior as far as the upper Skeena, and the Coast Tsimshian traded theirs to Kitkatla and to the Haida. Both groups bartered to the Tlingit who came to the Nass estuary. The Haida traded canoes, and after about 1830, potatoes, for olachen. The Tsimshian who had hereditary mountain-goat pastures traded wool, fat and horn for halibut, seal oil and seaweed. Though there are myth references to Coast Tsimshian village specialization in manufactures,[7] there is no evidence of such specialization in recent generations.

Many men supplemented the supplies collected by themselves and their families by specializing in woodcraft. Canoe builders, box makers, mask and pole carvers and men clever in the making of mechanical devices for dramatizations received food, clothing and other supplies for their manufactures. A pole carver and his family were often housed and fed by the chief for whom he worked until the pole was finished. Many shamans did no food collecting, depending on their fees in goods and food to satisfy the needs of themselves and their dependents.

Tsimshian women had much less opportunity than men to produce goods or services that were marketable. They could become shamans or compose songs for festivals. They could barter woven goods and preserved or fresh foods collected by themselves. Skilled blanket weavers could always command high prices for their wares. Adolescent daughters of wealthy families were not required to do any useful work. At puberty they were isolated for from several months to a year and spent their time in bored idleness.

Information on the actual work done by members of wealthy families is contradictory. Lineage and tribal heads were organizers and adminis-

---

[7] Boas, 1916, p. 398.

trators, receiving tribute in goods and services from their followers. They hunted sea lions and mountain goats, activities that required courage and endurance. However, according to Coast Tsimshian, chiefs usually directed the hunt and seldom participated in the danger or hard work of the actual drive. Tsimshian myths present the ideal lineage and tribal head as a man skilled in all things, energetic and ambitious. A frequent theme of mythology is of a chief's son or nephew who, through laziness or incompetence, brought shame and disgrace upon his family. There was probably a wide range of individual variability; some leaders worked along with their followers, others were organizers and directors, participating only when the activity was to their liking.

According to the custom in Northwest Coast matrilineal societies all resource properties belonged to lineages or their titular heads. However, the privilege of using areas belonging to a man were extended to his sons during his lifetime. A son could hunt, fish, trap or take anything he desired from any area where his father had hereditary rights. After his father's death a man discontinued the practice or asked permission of his father's successor; permission which was seldom denied. A son should take only what he needed for his own use and was criticized if commodities were utilized for a potlatch. The Tlingit were particularly critical of such a man, commenting that he fed guests from their own lands.

The right of sons stemmed from the fact that they grew up in their father's household, hunted and fished with him and learned many of their skills from him. Many adolescent boys took up residence with uncles, but permanent affiliation with their own lineages dated from marriage.

A man could invite his sons-in-law, his father-in-law or his wife's brothers to hunt or fish with him as guests. If they visited the areas without invitation they were regarded as trespassers. In cousin marriages, of course, a man's father-in-law was his uncle and the elder man's son-in-law was his own nephew.

A Tsimshian woman gathered everything she needed for her family's use from her husband's properties. She aided her own lineage head by working on the properties of her lineage or by borrowing from her husband. With her husband's consent she could pick berries from his lands and give them to a brother or uncle for his potlatch.[8] However, the recipient was obligated to return the loan at a later date. A Tsimshian man planning a large affair could borrow directly from his father or his wife's relatives or could request the use of their resource areas. Though this practice was known to the Tlingit and Haida they do not seem to have followed it as frequently as the Tsimshian.

[8] This is quite different from the Kwakiutl and Bella Coola ideas that a wife's family rebought her from the husband. See Boas, 1897a; McIlwraith, 1948, Vol. I, pp. 187—188.

CHAPTER TWO

SOCIAL ORGANIZATION

Phratries and Clans

The Tsimshian, Haida and Tlingit are unique among Northwest Coast societies for their complex matrilineal clan organization and exogamous phratries. Matrilineal clans were also present among some Athapascan speaking tribes, the Eyak of the Copper River delta, and the Heiltsuq and Kitimat of the northern Kwakiutl. Tribes adjacent to the Tsimshian and Tlingit show clear evidence of having borrowed their distinctive features of kinship structure and functioning, principally as the result of intermarriage. The Haida seem to have contributed little to this diffusion.

Moiety divisions are more widespread than other features of clan organization. They are known for most Athapascan tribes from Cook Inlet to Mackenzie River. They were also present in a few tribes of the northwestern Plateau which may have borrowed from Athapascan neighbors, and possibly in Alaskan Eskimo groups, though the evidence is not conclusive.

In some Athapascan tribes, moieties were composed of exogamous matrilineal divisions or clans. However, the Athapascans lacked the complex elaboration of house groups, lineages and clans of the Haida, Tlingit and Tsimshian, and rules of exogamy seem not to have been enforced by all Athapascans. Exogamy of the Kwakiutl was basically village exogamy, with the exception of the Heiltsuq and Kitimat, who had taken over the Tsimshian clan system. The Bella Coola guarded ancestral rights and property by imposing village endogamy. South and eastward of the Kwakiutl, marriage rules were imposed to prevent unions within the bilateral family and preferences for village exogamy stemmed from this idea or to cement inter-community friendships.

Everywhere in the Northwest mandatory, exogamy was linked with a belief in descent from common ancestors and an elaborate body of myths substantiating the belief. Tsimshian, Haida and Tlingit origin myths differed in one fundamental particular from those of the Kwakiutl and Bella Coola to the south of them, who reckoned descent through both parents but who also venerated ancestors. In tales of the first group, human or semi-divine ancestors settled a new village and established a new lineage which preserved relationship with the parent group through names, crests and myths. They were not true origin myths. Kwakiutl and Bella Coola tales most often began with the establishment of a village by a semi-divine sky being and continued with accounts of the

18

human descendants born and reared in the settlement. Thus, the Kwakiutl and Bella Coola stressed the tie between an ancestor, a locality and all descendants; the three northern tribes accented prerogatives obtained from ancestors and the shared experiences of each generation of descendants through the mothers. The name by which the descendants became known may originally have been the name of a camp or village site but it identified a lineage or clan, members of which were forbidden to marry.

Elements of a matrilineal complex have undoubtedly been introduced into the Northwest Coast from Asia. These probably included matrilineal descent with exogamy, totemistic beliefs and property control by the lineage.[1] It is not possible in the present stage of our knowledge to date the diffusion, nor to say with certainly which elements came together or singly. Whatever the facts revealed by further study, it is apparent that the greatest elaboration of the basic ideas was accomplished in the restricted area of southeastern Alaska and the coast of British Columbia south to Rivers Inlet, though matrilineal descent extended only to Gardner Channel.

The largest kinship division of the Tsimshian, Haida and Tlingit was a matrilineally traced, exogamous group. Various writers have termed it clan or phratry for the Tsimshian and clan or moiety for the dual divisions of the Haida and Tlingit. The phratry, the large and composite kinship division of this discussion, was a group of clans the members of which could not intermarry. The Tsimshian had four phratries. A few villages lacked representatives of one or two phratries.[2]

Coast Tsimshian and Nisqa phratries were commonly termed Eagles, Wolves, Ravens and Blackfish or Killerwhales. The Blackfish phratry was also referred to as the Bears, from a crest common to many of its subdivisions. The corresponding Gitksan phratries were called Eagles, Wolves, Frog-Raven and Fireweed. The native names of Eagles and Wolves can be literally translated "On the Eagle" and "On the Wolf." The etymology of Coast Tsimshian and Nisqa terms for the Ravens is unknown. It resembles the Tlingit name for their Raven phratry which means "The People of Ganax," a place name in southern Tlingit territory, probably in the vicinity of northern Prince of Wales Island. A number of Gitksan lineages of the Raven phratry regarded the Frog as their most significant crest. For this reason the phratry has been referred to as Frog-Raven by Dr. Barbeau,[3] but the Gitksan's own term for it was a place name, unrelated to the name applied to the division by the Nisqa and Coast Tsimshian. The Raven was a crest and identifying

---

[1] Birket-Smith and de Laguna, 1938, pp. 526—527.
[2] Boas, 1895, p. 50. There are only Raven and Wolf phratry members in Kitwinkool.
[3] Barbeau, 1929, p. 10.

symbol of nearly all lineages of the phratry both for the Tsimshian and for the equivalent phratry in tribes outside Tsimshian territory. No other phratry possessed a single crest with such wide distribution. The native name for the Blackfish phratry is untranslatable beyond the fact that it contains the prefix "people of." The Blackfish was one of the widely owned crests of the phratry. The Coast Tsimshian and Nisqa Blackfish group and the Gitksan Fireweed group were subdivisions of the same phratry for which there was no common native term. The Gitksan members called themselves "People of the Fireweed."

Phratries had no important function other than the regulation of spouse selection. They were essentially loose federations of clans, which were the named subdivisions of phratries. Each clan included people who shared legends, a history of common ancestors, and many crests, properties and privileges. The members of some clans within a phratry had little in common with other clans of the same phratry except the fact that they could not intermarry.

The composition of each phratry was extremely complex. Movements of people occurred out of neighboring non-Tsimshian areas and they joined, or were adopted into, one of the existing phratric subdivisions, or formed a new subdivision. There has also been considerable movement of Tsimshian within their own territory. Migrants had experiences and contacts not shared with relatives left behind and in time came to consider themselves as separate clans or lineages.

The following discussion is by no means a complete presentation of the origin and composition of Tsimshian phratries and clans, but illustrates their complexity.[4]

Legendary history of the clans of the Blackfish-Fireweed phratry shows their diversity of origin. One group of clans traced descent from Prairie Town, a mythical village occupied at the time of the Flood. Their principle crest was the Grizzly Bear, one of the supernatural powers gotten by an ancestor whose spirit quest beneath the lake caused the Flood. The Tsimshian regarded this group of clans as the oldest or original subdivision of the Blackfish-Fireweed phratry. Another main subdivision traced descent from the ancestress *Gau'o* or *Sqawo*, who married a Sky Being. Their descendants belonged to the Sky clans, whose crests referred to the adventures of their ancestress, her children and grandchildren. Most of the Sky clans also owned the Fireweed crest from which the Gitksan division of the phratry took its name. Sky clans were also represented among the Haida, Carrier and Babines.

Other Blackfish-Fireweed clans traced descent from a town outside China Hat, identified with the Bella Bella. Their Blackfish crest was derived from the legendary adventures of three ancestors in the home of Nagunaks, a supernatural being of the sea. When this monster discovered

[4] Barbeau, 1917; Boas, 1916, pp. 515—530.

that the men belonged to his Blackfish clan, he showered them with gifts and gave them permission to copy and use anything they heard or saw. An Eagle clansman was also in this party. He was given permission to tell the story and use the monster's name, and was given gifts for himself and his relatives. Therefore, some Eagle lineages also owned the Blackfish crest.

One subdivision of the Eagle phratry was called the Runaways or Fugitives. It traced its origin to the southern Tlingit and was represented in all three geographic divisions of the Tsimshian. The original members came from Copper River, where they had been vanquished by a Raven lineage. In the course of migrations, they acquired a Beaver hat, which is now the principle crest of descendants. Other subdivisions of clans of the Eagle phratry include one with Bella Bella affiliations and ownership of a Halibut crest, and another from the upper Skeena with Athapascan ancestors. The Eagles are represented in only one village of the Gitksan,[5] and in three of the four Nisqa tribal villages.[6]

The Wolf phratry of the Nisqa and Coast Tsimshian traced its main subdivisions from Tahltan ancestors who lived near the headwaters of the Stikine River. After a feud in which their leader was murdered, a number of brothers fled to the mouth of the Stikine where they were adopted by a local Tlingit chief. They gave him the personal names and prerogatives of their murdered uncle. A later quarrel caused at least some of the men to join the Tongass Tlingit, where they left various possessions, including the tale of their misfortunes and adventures. After a quarrel at Tongass one of the men went to the Nass where a Nisqa chief adopted him as a nephew. He presented his new uncle with the names of his murdered Tahltan relatives. He also told the full story of his and his brothers' adventures, including their escape down the Stikine by paddling along a stream that ran under a glacier. The adventures of the men of the Tahltan Wolf phratry seem to have ended with the settlement on the Nass. The spread of their descendants to other Tsimshian villages was peaceful. According to one version of their legendary history, the migration from Tongass was two-fold; one group settled on the Nass, another on the lower Skeena. The ancestors of other clans of the Wolf phratry, represented in Tahltan, Tlingit and Tsimshian villages, did not participate in these adventures. The Wolf phratry is numerically weak in all three of the Tsimshian geographic areas, but is represented in Qaldo, the northernmost town.[7]

---

[5] Barbeau, 1929, pp. 133—143. In Kitwanga, the southernmost Gitskan village.

[6] Sapir, 1915, p. 4.

[7] Barbeau, 1929, p. 147. The Fireweed phratry is also represented at Qaldo. There are Fireweed and Wolf phratry members at Kisgasas, but not Eagle and Raven. These are the two most northerly Tsimshian towns.

The Raven or Frog-Raven phratry is represented in Nisqa and Coast Tsimshian by several subdivisions.[8] One derived its ancestry from the Tlingit of Cape Fox. Another came from the interior. Ancestors of some Gitksan clans of the Frog-Raven phratry came from the Nass, others from the Haida of the Queen Charlotte Islands. Ancestors of the Waterlily clan were Hagwelget of Bulkeley River canyon. Ancestors of the Wild-rice clan were nomadic Tsetsaut bands from the headwaters of the Skeena River. Coast Tsimshian of the Raven phratry who claim Haida ancestors are of two groups. One claims special crests because some of its ancestors settled in Haida country after the Flood. Present members descended from children of an ancestress who returned to the Nass with her offspring. Another group, the Tongue-licked clans, are descended from a Coast Tsimshian woman who was captured by the Haida and married to a chief. After the birth of her son she murdered her husband, took his head as a trophy, and went to Nass with her baby. The boy grew up to be a fearless warrior who terrorized the Tsimshian and their neighbors. Crests and other prerogatives of the group were derived from the escape of the woman and from her son's war adventures.

House Groups and Lineages

In theory, all members of a clan were obligated to render mutual assistance and protection. The members were in fact scattered so widely over Tsimshian territory and beyond that many did not know of one another's existence. People who functioned as a group were only the members of that closely related segment of a clan which is termed a house group or lineage.

Tsimshian terms for this group, whose reckoning was matrilineal, may be translated as "relatives," or as "people of the house."[9] Though the house group or lineage, like the clan, included some people who were relatives only by rationalization, most of those who lived, worked and potlatched under the leadership of an hereditary head were biological kin. From the point of view of an individual, those with whom he associated most and to whom he had the greatest obligation included his brothers, sisters, mother's brothers and sisters, the children of his mother's sisters, and the children of their daughters. Depending on circumstances, the group might also include the children of his mother's mother's sisters and daughters. The oldest man in the lineage was usually head of the group and custodian of all its economically important property.

Such property included food producing areas such as halibut and codfish banks, stretches of beach and sections of streams, hunting terri-

[8] Sapir, 1915, p. 4. Ravens are represented in three of the four Nisqa tribes.
[9] Garfield, 1939, pp. 173—174.

tories, berry grounds, and dwellings. The house group also owned totem poles, ceremonial paraphernalia and other carved and painted objects. These illustrated legends or historical accounts of the experiences and exploits of ancestors. The right to relate and dramatize such tales was enjoyed only by lineage members. House and personal names were also lineage property. Many of these names were derived from, or referred to, ancestral experiences with human and supernatural beings. Lineage prerogatives also included guardian spirit powers revealed to ancestors.

All these property rights were under the supervision and administration of the male head of the lineage. The dwelling was known by the hereditary name of the house head, and each succeeding candidate for the position assumed the name, and the properties, duties and privileges that went with the name. Tsimshian genealogies are difficult to unravel because of the custom of continuing personal names from generation to generation.

Since marriages between members of the same phratry were forbidden, a man and his wife belonged to two of the four phratries and, of course, to different clans and lineages. Children belonged to the kinship group of their mother. They were members of her lineage, and consequently were members of her clan and phratry. A married woman lived with her husband, hence in a home that belonged to his lineage. Husbands and wives could not inherit from each other, nor could children inherit from their fathers. Although children were raised in their father's house, they spent much time in the houses of their mother's brothers. This was especially so for boys, who were to take an active part in the affairs of their own lineage when they had grown up. Girls spent most of their early years in their father's home and, upon marriage, in the home of their husband. Only during brief visits did they live in a house which belonged to their own lineage. When a woman left her husband, it was customary for her to return to her father's house if her parents were living. Otherwise she went to the home of a brother or of her mother's brother.

Marriage

The ideal marriage, indicated time and again in Tsimshian mythology, was between a man and the daughter of his mother's brother. From a girl's point of view the ideal husband was the son of her father's sister. If a survey of marriages of living persons is indicative, it suggests that in former times only a small percentage of marriages conformed to the ideal. However, if we include marriages which occured between persons who could trace descent from a common grandparent or great-grandparent, the number of ideal marriages between relatives is increased. Cousin marriage bound the two lineages in ties of affection, consolidated hereditary property, and extended the privileges of use of resources,

Marriages were contractual arrangements between lineages. They ex-pressed personal friendships, political exigencies and interests in the maintainance of wealth and social position. Young people had little to say since romantic love was not regarded as a basis for marriage. Nego-tiations were conducted by mothers or grandmothers; the initiative was usually taken by the boy's relatives. Gifts were taken by the boy's emissary to the relatives of the girl and the proposal made. After the several weeks or months demanded by etiquette, some of the girl's relatives came to the boy's home with gifts. If the arrangements were satisfactory, the exchange of gifts constituted a marital contract.

The wedding was usually celebrated at the home of the groom, who lived with his father or one of his uncles. Gifts were again exchanged between the in-laws and food and gifts were provided for guests. The wedding was a celebration for everyone but the principals, who sat quietly in the center of the house and otherwise took no part. Speeches were made by relatives, who vied in the recital of their family histories. Songs, dances and dramatic skits entertained the guests and re-impressed them with the importance of lineage possessions.

Following the wedding day the couple set up housekeeping. The young wife was under the supervision of her husband's uncle's wife. The groom continued his participation in the affairs of the household under his uncle's guidance. The fathers of the couple had little part in the premarital or postmarital proceedings. Nonetheless, they were deeply concerned that their children should make good marriages. Probably they exerted more influence than is evident from a formal description of customs as given by native informants. In cousin marriages, the father of the bride was also uncle of the groom and, therefore, more pointedly involved.

The Tsimshian regarded marriage as a permanent arrangement. Relatives tried to keep incompatible couples together. But if the couple separated, each was free to marry again. Children went with the mother.

The husband of a childless woman could divorce her or demand a second wife from among her relatives. The concept of a contract between lineages was further emphasized by the fact that death of the wife during the early years of marriage obligated her relatives to provide a substitute. The responsibility for support of the wives and children of a deceased man fell on the shoulders of his levirate successor. He either married the widow, or if he consented she might marry some other man. The custom of inheriting wives sometimes resulted in young men acquiring elderly wives, and in very young women being married to middle-aged and elderly men. Such customs continue in a few Tsimshian families today. The levirate stabilized reciprocal relationships between lineages and guaranteed that no widow was left destitute. If she had small children, she had less to worry about than have widowed mothers of our own society. Since the successor was most often a nephew or brother who was already living in the house, there was a minimum of household re-organization. The only important source of friction was a younger man's wife who aspired to leadership among the women of the household; the danger was that she would usurp the position of the older woman who had held authority. The chief's first or senior wife was looked up to as the woman with most authority over women, children and slaves in the household.

Reciprocal duties of the in-law lineages were brought into prominence at the birth of a child. It was the privilege of the husband's sister to serve as midwife, and of his brother to furnish the cradle board. The mother later invited her sister-in-law and presented her with baskets, clothing and other gifts. If the mother was a member of a wealthy lineage, she, her brothers, and sisters gave a feast and invited her husband's brothers, sisters and other relatives; gifts were presented to all the guests. The baby was named at this or a later feast of the same kind. The announcement of the name was made by a member of the child's father's lineage, though the name itself was chosen from names that belonged to the mother's lineage. However simple or elaborate the affair, there was a formal compensation paid to the child's father's relatives for their services and for announcing its name. A child was not regarded as a properly registered member of the community until such an announcement had been made.

As the child grew, its father and its mother's brother were equally concerned about its welfare. Each step in its progress was marked with a feast or other public announcement of its accomplishments.

All children had at least one hole in the helix of the ear for ornaments. Girls had a similar hole in the lower lip for insertion of a labret. Only slaves and children of very poor families grew up without these adornments. Daughters of wealthy families had as many as four holes in each ear. They and their brothers were sometimes tattooed with lineage crests. Each operation was performed for the child by a member of its father's lineage at a public ceremony. Invited guests were feasted, entertained and presented with gifts. In addition, every child was presented to the protective supernatural spirits, usually under the auspices of the chief. Children of Nisqa and Coast Tsimshian families were also initiated into one of the two secret societies or magical treasure clubs.

Such initiations were sponsored by the child's father or by his mother's brother, though a man never sponsored his own children and his nieces and nephews at the same affair. The last public affair which a father sponsored for his daughter was her post-pubescent party at which he announced that she was ready for marriage.

Adolescent boys usually lived with their uncles who took full responsibility for advancing them in the social scale. During childhood affectional bonds between fathers and children seem to have been close and fathers took as much pride as uncles in the progress of children.

Death again called forth the reciprocity of kinship groups, whose duties and obligations were well defined. When a death occurred, brothers and sisters of the deceased's father were immediately called. To the men was delegated the task of funeral arrangements and to the women the care of the corpse and supervision of mourning. The funeral of the head of a house or of a tribe was often a very elaborate affair, while that of a child, a woman or poor man was much simpler. However simple or elaborate, the persons who performed services in connection with the funeral were later compensated at a potlatch.

To summarize: there were two principal categories of reciprocal obligations; those between kin, real and putative, and those between an individual and his or her father's relatives. A third set of obligations existed between spouses, and between the relatives of spouses, a part of which stemmed from their mutual interest in the welfare and social progress of the children of the couple.

Class and Rank

The Tsimshian shared with other peoples of the coast from California northward a high regard for owners of wealth and the practice of its hereditary transmission to legally designated successors. Wealth on the entire coast was in slaves, accumulated stores of food, manufactured goods, and, in the northern part of the area which includes the Tsimshian, a larger percentage of what was produced from the strategic resources of lands and waters. Management of Tsimshian resource areas and distribution of the products derived from them was in the hands of lineage heads and tribal chiefs. These were the principal owners of wealth. Their positions were hereditary, and both they and their heirs belonged to the upper class. There were approximately thirty tribal chiefs in the Nisqa, Gitksan and Coast Tsimshian, and a very much larger number of lineage and house heads. Since successors were normally chosen from among brothers and eldest sisters's sons, they also belonged to the upper class, as did their mothers and wives. The closeness of such men to the headmen meant an advantage over the descendants of younger sisters and their daughters. Sons of the latter could not expect to rise to positions of leadership and influence unless all heirs in the direct line died or were disqualified. Such chances were extremely small.

Inheritance of wealth in addition to the power which accompanied its acquirement and manipulation tended to set Tsimshian house heads and their heirs apart from the rest of their lineage relatives and to concentrate control of wealth in the hands of a few men. They manipulated economically valuable resources or property, directed production and other work, controlled distribution of major production, and had political authority. The heads of all lineages and houses shared these advantages and therefore formed a group with common interests, which were class interests. Such leaders had power to bestow hereditary names, privileges and other lineage prerogatives on relatives of their choosing. Since every bestowal must be accompanied by a potlatch, and the head controlled the people, resources and accumulations necessary for giving one, he had the power to select recipients of even hereditary privileges. A few generations of such selection concentrated the properties and prerogatives in the line of descent of older brothers and their older nephews.

A tribal chief had much more wealth, both hereditary and on demand from his followers, than any lineage leader. He also had much more patronage to distribute. In addition, tribal chiefs had certain exclusive rights not shared with lineage heads. They received tribute in food and goods from all tribal members, including trade goods and potlatch gifts. Tribal chiefs and the members of their lineages were especially privileged upper class men and women to whom unique deference was paid. They had wealth and power not available to any other members of their tribes.

Status and personality traits of a tribal chief were noted both implicitly and explicitly in the myths and tales, as well as in ethnographic interviews. A chief must be well-born. No taint of slave ancestry should mar his record. An unblemished genealogy was one in which all of a chief's remembered ancestors were the sons and daughters of chiefs. Chiefs should be able leaders, good speakers, haughty and proud before strangers, and humble and generous toward tribesmen. The ideal leader was an able organizer and speaker, and a model of good taste and conduct. Above all, a chief must be able to command wealth and to distribute it to the benefit of his tribesmen and to the renown of his people and himself. A popular folkloristic motif treats of the man who acquired great wealth through supernatural aid, fed his tribe and became a great chief, and was loved by all his people. Quite properly he married the daughter of his uncle, the former chief, and they carried on the noble line. Tribal chiefs were conscious of their high rank and of the common interests and prerogatives which set them off from their followers. Formal ranking in potlatch seating and gift distribution centered on the relative ranking of tribal chiefs. Lineage heads, their heirs and other relatives were ranked in relation to the chiefs of the tribes to which they belonged. Hence it is incorrect to assume that individual guests at a Tsimshian potlatch were seated in order from highest to lowest rank. The seating of commoners was dependent upon where the chiefs sat. Ranking of these chiefs varied according to the relation of guest chiefs to the host. If the host and guest chief were of the same clan, the guest was treated as a relative and he and his tribesmen occupied seats with other such relatives. Seating and order of receiving gifts was, therefore, not from high to low but varied with the occasion. The ability of a Tsimshian to list the order of guests in any given circumstance does not mean that there was a fixed sequence in rank. Much less does it imply a lack of class differences or distinctions.[10]

Tsimshian class distinctions were especially sharp in the status accorded chiefs. Distinctions were only less sharply marked for other classes. Class was a matter of birth. Apart from the chiefs as such, their families enjoyed participation in cultural activities different from those not so favored by heredity. Lineage heads and their relatives were set apart, on the one hand, from tribal chiefs and chiefs' relatives and, on the other hand, from people who were only distant relatives of lineage heads. The large number of lineages and the lack of rigid rules of primogeniture prevented lineage heads, their close kin and heirs from forming as distinct a class as would have been the case had there been strict succession of the eldest.

The descendants of junior lines, the children of younger sisters and their daughters could not hope to succeed to positions of leadership. Their only opportunity for prestige and social participation was through the leaders of their lineages. They helped accumulate goods for pot- latches but received only insignificant gifts when invited. A substantial part of a chief's expendable wealth came from them in the form of contributions of provisions, manufactured goods and labor. They were formally ranked at potlatches in relation to tribal chiefs and lineage heads. Such formal ranking amounted to seating position, and order of serving of food and receipt of gifts.

Perhaps more than their neighbors the Tsimshian recognized the im- portance of women in the maintainance of class and rank. This recog- nition was exhibited both in the initiation of women into secret societies and in provisions for giving them hereditary dancing powers belonging to their lineages. Women and girls were also presented at potlatches; there they were given names and property was distributed to guests on their behalf. Women of the chief class took tribal chiefs' names, at least in the nineteenth century if not earlier. Two Coast Tsimshian chief- tainesses who came to power because there were no close male heirs were influential leaders. Their abilities and personalities were respected. One was the sister of the deceased chief and the other was a niece. A third woman worth noting took over leadership of a lineage when her brother refused; she ably managed its affairs until her son grew up. She then initiated a potlatch at which he assumed the name and responsibilities. There is no recorded instance where a Haida or Tlingit group solved the problem of a successor by choosing a woman.

[10] Drucker, 1939.

In every tribe and village there were poor people who lived with or were regarded as part of a chief's household. They ranked only above slaves. They were often described as "those without origin" or as people without relatives. They had no lineage heads and no hereditary lands. They constituted a class which worked for the chief and in return received protection and subsistence.

Slaves were the lowest class. The Northwest Coast is the one well documented example of an area in which food gatherers kept and exploited slaves.

The Tsimshian either bought slaves, especially from southern tribes, or captured them in raids. They raided Kwakiutl villages and those of their Athapascan-speaking neighbors. Haida and Tlingit captives were also taken. They were not averse to raiding other Tsimshian towns, especially if so distant as to lessen the danger of reprisal. The only precaution observed when raiding was that a person of the same phratry as the captor was not held as a slave. But a raider was willing to exchange a captive phratric relative for a non-relative, or to allow one of his companions to take the phratric-related captive. This custom applied to any group with a phratry organization and also to nearby Athapascans who had only a clan organization.

Persons reduced to slavery lost all family, lineage, clan or phratric affiliations and their descendants were slaves. Marriages between free persons and slaves were forbidden, though chiefs sometimes married captured women of high birth. Chiefs had slave concubines and wealthy women occasionally had slave paramours. Children of concubines were of slave status unless their fathers chose to adopt them as nieces or nephews in a formal adoption ceremony. There were no formal marriage ceremonies for slaves. If a couple belonged to the same master, they lived together. Children belonged to the owner of the mother.

Owners had complete power over the lives and persons of slaves. Slaves lived and worked with members of families and performed menial, monotonous and disagreeable tasks. Men slaves fished, loaded, unloaded, paddled and cared for canoes. They helped build canoes and houses. They made tools and assisted in all other tasks that did not require specialized training. Women slaves prepared fish and other foods for drying, made oil, collected mat and basket materials and berries, and assisted with other household tasks. Chiefs, their heirs, wives and children also had personal servants who accompanied them and waited on them. Young slaves were assigned to chiefs' sons and daughters as companions and bodyguards.

In addition to the slaves who were kept by wealthy families as workers and personal servants, many others were purchased as a part of the property accumulated for distribution at a potlatch. It was profitable to convert perishable or bulky provisions, goods, and even blankets into

slaves when preparing for a potlatch or other public affair. A slave's la-
bors added to the store of potlatch goods and he himself was wealth to be
given away. In this fashion he paid for the cost of acquiring him.

Like their neighbors, the Tsimshian emphasized the prestige value
of slave owning in their oral traditions and accounts of potlatches. It
was not a part of the culture pattern to collect and publicize data on
economic production either by freemen or slaves. The culture emphasized
only the products that were gifts. The chiefs and headmen did not
concern themselves with an inventory of the number of fish dried by a
family during a summer or the man-hours required for the making of a
blanket or carving of a totem pole. Accurate count was made only of the
gifts granted each potlatch recipient. These gifts were presented in the
name of the host, or in the names of certain of his relatives or sub-
ordinates who were honored during the potlatch. Certainly no host
credited slaves with contributing to his wealth. But he boasted about
the high prices he had paid for them, and the number he was able to
give away. Slaves were the most expensive potlatch gifts. Their mone-
tary value during the nineteenth century varied from two hundred to a
thousand dollars.

Some ethnographers have emphasized the prestige value of slaves as
an index of their economic worth. There are also assertions that slaves
were of no economic value but were kept only for the prestige owners
derived from their possession.[11] Points of view such as these can be
accounted for only because of the absence of adequate field description
of the role and status of slaves and the ethnographers' disregard of the
productive work of slaves. Slaves worked with family members and not
at tasks exclusively reserved for them and what they produced was
pooled as part of the families' stores of goods. It is, therefore, difficult to
segregate slave production from that of freemen. In spite of the diffi-
culties, such studies should be made in order to provide a fuller understanding of basic features of the economy of the area.

The economic role of slave labor must have been very important,
apart from the undoubted prestige accruing to their owners. Ten to
twenty slaves are reported as belonging to each of the nine tribal chiefs
of Port Simpson in the middle nineteenth century. Each of approximately fifty Port Simpson lineage heads is also reported to have owned
from two to as many as ten slaves. These slaves certainly did much
more than earn their subsistence or give prestige to their owners.[12]

Another aspect of Northwest Coast culture which tied in with the
pattern of slave holding was kidnapping. Members of wealthy families
were selected, kidnapped and held for ransom. This was a quick and

[11] Barnett, 1938, p. 352.
[12] MacLeod, 1928, p. 639.

profitable way of acquiring wealth, or of disgracing and vanquishing an enemy, although it was attended with the danger of retaliation. When an agreement was reached with the captive's relatives, the ransom was paid and he was released. The captive and his relatives had to give a potlatch to remove the stigma of temporary bondage. War captives could be redeemed in the same way. In either case, unredeemed captives and their descendants became slaves.

CHAPTER THREE

POLITICAL ORGANIZATION

One of the characteristics of Northwest Coast societies is the extreme simplicity of formal political organization. Power over, and responsibility for, members of a house, lineage, or village were in the hands of the man who administered the economic resources of the group and by the same token owned the most wealth. The minimal political unit of the Haida, Tlingit and Tsimshian was the local segment of each clan that lived in one or more houses. There were several such units in each village. Only rarely did the authority of a lineal head extend beyond his lineage relatives in his own village.

Haida villages seem originally to have been settled and owned by lineage heads, and a Haida village was therefore, in origin, identical with a house group or local lineage segment of a clan. Villages of the Haida continued to be identified with the lineages of their first settlers, though they grew and later contained houses that belonged to a number of different clans and to both phratries. The head of the senior house, who was a male descendant of the first settlers, was known as the "village mother" or "village master." He had jurisdiction only over his own relatives. His position of seniority in social status gave him an advantage which he exercised in advising other house heads, especially in matters that concerned the village as a whole.[1]

Like the Haida, many Tlingit villages stemmed from very small groups which settled in unoccupied spots and built one or two houses. According to native accounts the sites of several towns were selected by founders who were later joined by brothers-in-law and friends with their families. Some sites were camps which later became permanent settlements. The Tlingit never developed a political headship beyond that of the house group, and villages continued to be made up of independent lineages each of which was presided over by a headman or chief. Lineage heads did not have equal prestige and influence. The main advantage one chief had over the others developed when his house group outnumbered the members of the other lineages and so attained greater wealth. A man who presided over several houses as the senior head commanded more wealth and had more influence than one who had only the members of a single house under his jurisdiction. Some lineages were traditionally of higher rank than others and the influence of their headmen was increased by the advantage of birth.

[1] Murdock, 1934.

Tsimshian political organization was basically similar to the Tlingit and Haida. House heads had authority only over their own relatives, whose personal and property rights they protected. Tsimshian villages, like those of the Tlingit and Haida were usually named from some geographic feature, not from the kinship groups which founded them. The first settlers established rights to ownership of economically strategic resources within reach of their settlement. Late comers were either assigned portions of areas not needed, or took up claims to unused areas. Some of the newcomers belonged to clans and phratries different from those of the old settlers. Others were house and lineage relatives who owed allegiance to the founders.

However, the Tsimshian of the lower Skeena and Nass Rivers are unique. They developed lineage political leadership into village chieftainship, probably early in the eighteenth century. Before the beginning of the nineteenth century this had developed further into tribal chieftainship. As far as we know they had the only overall tribal organization headed by a chief that was found in northwestern North America. If there were other such chieftainships in the area, they have not yet been satisfactorily described.

There were nine main tribal villages on the lower one hundred and fifty miles of the Skeena River below the canyon and four on the lower Nass. The Skeena villages were settled principally by people who had moved down from the interior along the river and its tributaries. It was in these villages that the dominance of the head of one lineage crystallized into village chieftainship. The chief of a village continued as hereditary head of his own lineage. This transformation from headship over members of a group of kin to chief of a local village was effected before the arrival of Europeans and before the location of permanent settlements on the channels between the shores of Tsimshian Peninsula and the present town of Prince Rupert, collectively called Metlakatla.

The original settlement generally referred to as Metlakatla was actually a cluster of nine independent villages, each composed of descendants of settlers from Skeena River towns.[2] Previous to permanent removal to Metlakatla residents of Skeena villages had camped there on their way to and from the olachen fishing grounds of the Nass. Each Skeena village had its own site which was hereditary property. The village chief camped approximately in the center of the site, with the camps of his heirs and leading lineage heads on either side. Other villagers built permanent or temporary structures along the beach beyond those of their leaders. Gradually, families took up permanent residence. Emigrants from each Skeena town settled as a separate unit

---

[2] Metlakatla means Salt Water Channel. A mission was built on the site of one of the old villages in 1862 and christened Metlakatla. The villagers moved to Alaska in 1887 and named their town New Metlakatla.

and continued to call themselves by the name of their former village, though they gave a new name to their new town. Permanent settlements were established before 1800 but the towns on the Skeena were not abandoned. Chiefs of the Skeena villages appointed representatives from among their heirs to take over chieftainships in the new villages. A few senior chiefs emigrated and left leadership of the old villages in the hands of successors. In either case, senior chiefs continued to exercise authority over the younger men, at least in the early period of the splitting of villages. At this stage tribal chieftainship emerged and the tribal chief was regarded as the active leader of his tribesmen regardless of where they lived. As permanent villages became established at Metlakatla, they received additional residents from Alaska, the Nass, the Queen Charlotte Islands, and the mainland and islands to the south. Expansion of the Tsimshian was resisted by the Tlingit with whom they engaged in feuds over rights to the coast between the Skeena and Nass estuaries.

Another camping place on the way to and from the Nass was the site now occupied by Port Simpson, about twenty miles north of Metlakatla on the mainland. The same pattern of hereditary beach camp sites was maintained at Port Simpson as at Metlakatla and the spot was used by Skeena River people before they settled permanently at Metlakatla. In 1834, the Hudson's Bay Company built a post on the native site at Port Simpson. Within a few years, the Skeena River and Metlakatla towns were virtually abandoned and the people reassembled on the hereditary tribal camping grounds in the middle of which the Fort was built. By 1935, segregation of tribal villages had been almost obliterated due to breakdown of native customs of house ownership and inheritance. The functions and power of lineage heads and tribal chiefs had also been destroyed. A few chiefs still held office, especially where tribal resource holdings were advantageous to them.

Information on the details of development of village and tribal chieftainship on the Nass is meager, but we know that there were four tribal villages on the lower seventy-five miles of the Nass River, each headed by a chief.[3] The Nisqa and Coast Tsimshian shared the same kinship structure and the same high regard for wealth and noble birth. The Coast Tsimshian tribes had permanent camps at the olachen fishing grounds to which they returned yearly and were in close touch with the Nisqa with whom they exchanged spouses and potlatches. The Coast Tsimshian introduced secret society dances to the Nisqa and it seems likely that they also influenced their political development.

The Gitksan did not have the wealth of the coastal tribes and therefore did not place so much emphasis on chiefs' positions. They had no

[3] Sapir, 1915.

tribal chiefs. Their attitudes were also affected by their proximity to, and relationships with, Athapascan tribes.

The tribal chieftainships of the Coast Tsimshian and Nisqa were superimposed upon earlier lineage headships. Obligations which previously existed between lineage heads and kin were duplicated between tribal chiefs and followers, and property concepts formerly applied to lineages were extended to tribal chiefs. Lineages owned property; tribes also owned resource areas, homes, house furnishings and treasure valuables for their chiefs, who, within limits, administered tribal property for the glory of themselves and their subjects. With slight alterations, the whole body of customs pertaining to lineage chieftainship was transferred to tribal headships. Tribes provided their chiefs with slaves and luxuries such as copper shields, Chilkat blankets, copper ornaments and richly ornamented chests, dishes and spoons. A part of everything acquired or made was presented to him, whether a catch of seals or fish, a choice cut of bear meat, or trade goods. He also collected tribute of trade goods from his tribesmen. In the middle nineteenth century, one chief at Port Simpson claimed exclusive monopoly of trade between upper Skeena River and the Fort and he levied a tax on all barter goods transported along the river. Trading trips up the river were conducted under his supervision or that of one of his own clansmen.

Little or no formal political authority was granted to the tribal chief. He was given no power to either enforce or change customary law, nor to intervene in disputes between tribal members unless asked to use his persuasive powers to bring about a settlement. He could council, threaten, cajole, but not command any but the members of his own lineage. In actual practice, a tribal chief was not a man whose wishes could be lightly disregarded. He had great wealth and an illustrious name; he had patronage to distribute and slaves and young men at his command to work for him; he could mobilize an armed guard or a raiding party larger than was available to any lineage head. Chiefs could and did quell resistance by armed force when necessary.

Lineage heads within the village or tribe formed the tribal chief's council. It organized the members of all the lineages for tribal undertakings such as a chief's potlatch, the building of a new house for him, the burial of a chief, and the installation of a successor. The council advised him on the selection of wives and of a successor. It decided whether tribal wealth should be invested in slaves, copper shields or potlatches. Since the chief could not promote any extensive undertaking without the council's approval and aid, it had an effective defense against dictatorial tactics, a defense which councils did not always choose to use.

The tribal chief's office, like that of the lineage head, was inherited by a brother or a sister's son. The council was influential in the selection of an heir because it could refuse to support anyone of whom it disapproved, and could prevent him from using the chief's home or wealth. During the period of cultural disintegration in the nineteenth century there were several instances of the exercise of veto rights by councils at Port Simpson. In one case, the council refused to finance the painting of the chief's house, and later refused to build him a new one. In another case, members would not allow the chief to sell the home which the council maintained was tribal, and not private, property.

The death of a chief involved great expense and drew every member of the tribe into participation. As in the death of a lineage head or commoner, funeral arrangements were made and carried out by the chief's father's lineage relatives, though they usually appointed other chiefs to perform honorary services. Every member of the tribe was expected to contribute toward expenses of the funeral and the later potlatch at which the successor took office. Members of the dead chief's clan were expected to be especially liberal in their giving; fellow chiefs of the same phratry also contributed. The successor inherited all the possessions of the deceased, and he and his lineage made the largest contribution to expenses. Neighboring tribes or villages were invited to the funeral, which ended with a feast and distribution of gifts by the heir, who announced his intention to take the position at a commemorative inaugural potlatch to be given at a later date. In the meantime, he functioned as acting chief, but he would not be addressed by the chief's name until his formal installation.

Preparations for inauguration of the new chief often took several years and were under the direction of the heir and council, who planned and allotted the tasks. Lineage heads were responsible for organizing the collections of foods and manufacture of articles by their relatives. Artists, stage set designers, song composers, and dancers planned dramatic presentations of lineage and tribal history under the supervision of the new chief. The potlatch was a round of feasting, entertaining and visiting, with the installation of the heir the culminating event.[4] Property was distributed, part of which was in payment of debts owed by the deceased man and incurred in connection with his funeral.

A chief's privileges and responsibilities were many. He decided when the tribe should leave for seasonal fishing, and he sent scouts to note the run of fish. The work of slaves and of poor men without relatives was planned and directed by him. Young men were subject to call for any task the chief wanted done. They served as the chief's messengers, carriers, scouts and army. He organized camp and work parties or designated competent leaders. He utilized an armed show of strength to

[4] Tsimshian potlatches are described by Boas, 1916, pp. 537—542; Garfield, 1939, pp. 192—219. For a general discussion of potlatching see Murdock, 1936; Barnett, 1938; and Drucker, 1939.

prevent attacks on his tribesmen or to avenge wrongs against them. Able-bodied men were recruited from his own tribe and volunteers were sought from friendly tribes. He retained the larger part of the booty from raids organized by him, and he apportioned a lesser part among his armed followers. Some of the booty from raids organized by other tribesmen was given to the chief as his just due.

No potlatch or secret society initiation could be given by a tribal member until the chief had officially opened the winter ceremonial season. His affairs took priority over those sponsored by lineage heads, who must provide him with wealth before they were able to accumulate for their own potlatches.

Certain other prerogatives of chiefs were also a source of wealth. No Coast Tsimshian child could be initiated into a secret society or presented at a potlatch until a throwing dance had been given for it. The throwing of a spirit into a child during the ceremony could only be done by a chief, who was handsomely compensated. No lineage head could give a potlatch without inviting the tribal chief, who received the largest gifts even though he took no active part. If he were asked to take part, he received an even larger gift.

A chief gained friends and allies in other tribes by his own judicious marriage to daughters or nieces of other chiefs. His control of the armed force of his tribe made opposition by other chiefs difficult and gained for him additional wealth due to the acquisition of slaves and booty taken in raids. His command of a large number of slaves and of the working time of young men of the tribe were major factors in the enhancement of his economic position, while his right to fees and gifts at potlatches and secret society initiations further increased his wealth and power.

CHAPTER FOUR

SUPERNATURAL POWERS

Guardian Spirit Power

Belief in guardian spirit powers was as fundamental an ideological feature in Tsimshian culture as it was in the cultures of most other tribes of North America and northeastern Asia.[1] The most widely distributed guardian spirit practices in North America were those associated with vision quests by shamans, whose tutelary powers served mainly in the diagnosis and cure of disease. Also widely distributed was the layman's solitary quest for supernatural assistance in day-to-day activities of hunting, fishing, feuding, love making and acquisition of wealth. In most tribes, supernatural powers acquired by shamans were regarded as more dangerous or potent than those acquired for other than shaman-istic purposes. Though there were usually no tabus against women becoming shamans, the most famous and successful were men. Women seldom acquired hunting, war or wealth powers.

The belief that a supernatural power could be inherited, or that a supernatural being or force gave power to successive generations of relatives, was weakly developed except on the Pacific Northwest Coast. Elsewhere, the belief was that an individual had a better chance of receiving assistance from an ancestor's power than he did from an independent source, but there appears to have been no clear-cut concept of inheritance of spirit power.

The tribes of the northern part of the Northwest Coast derived the greater number of their powers from hereditary sources. This was especially true of the Tlingit, Haida, Kwakiutl, Bella Coola, Nootka and Tsimshian, and to a lesser extent of their immediate neighbors who show evidences of extensive borrowing of features of culture from one or several of the above groups. The Kwakiutl and Nootka stressed the transmission of hereditary powers through the secret societies, though some powers were acquired in potlatches. The Tlingit, Haida and Tsimshian emphasized transmission of lineage and house group prerog-atives in potlatches; among these prerogatives was the right to receive powers from the supernatural guardians of ancestors. Secret society dances and prerogatives, acquired by these three groups from the northern Kwakiutl, were generally fitted into the already existing pattern of transmission of hereditary privileges within narrowly limited lineages.

[1] Benedict, 1923.

In the tales of all tribes who shared the belief in guardian spirit aides, there were accounts of persons who acquired spirit assistance without apparent effort. In the stories, the orphan, slave or poor boy, the widow or deserted child received help from supernaturals or their agencies. Aided by a gift of magical weapons or extraordinary skills the poor and the oppressed became wealthy and influential.[2] There were also a few tales in which the recipient of supernatural benefits was an undistinguished citizen, neither more nor less ambitious than his fellows, who came in contact with supernaturals while hunting or traveling. Though some of these were merely adventure stories, the men were given tokens to prove that the creatures they encountered were not of the ordinary variety.

The Tsimshian regarded spirit power acquisition and protection as essential for all free persons. Children's training in bathing and occasional fasting was the first step. The throwing dance in which chiefs called upon one or another of their spirits and threw the power into a child was the second essential step. From there on differences of sex, lineage wealth, hereditary rank, and interests correlated with many differences in the kind and number of spirit aides adults received.

A Tsimshian candidate who sought power followed a prescribed routine of bathing, fasting, taking a purgative, continence and solitude, though the procedure was also used for purposes other than the direct acquisition of a guardian power. In some instances, it seems to have been used as a kind of magical formula or ritual where correct performance automatically brought about a desired result.

Ritual bathing by boys was regarded by the Tsimshian as essential to make them strong and hardy. Supervised by their fathers and uncles, all boys in a village were required to take a daily early morning dip regardless of the weather. Winter bathing was believed to be especially beneficial. Switches of spruce boughs or salmon berry canes were used to beat the boys, who were admonished not to cry or complain. After a dip or swim, they were taken into the houses to stand by the fire and drink olachen grease. Supervised bathing was continued for a period following puberty. Girls received the same training as boys before puberty, particularly if their relatives wished them to become shamans or to be strong and hardy. At the appearance of the first menses, they were isolated and tended by older women relatives who supervised their training.

Before a hunting trip, Tsimshian men went through a period of training, including bathing, which was especially stressed for mountain-goat, bear and sea-lion hunting, or to assure success where conditions were dangerous or game scarce. The formulae used in such ceremonial bathing varied. Some formulae were closely guarded secrets revealed to ancestors

[2] Randall, 1949.

and taught by uncles to nephews. Others were probably based on hunting lore which, if successful, were passed on to younger men. Men who prepared to take an hereditary power or name, or to be initiated into a secret society, also bathed. So did persons who desired to acquire shamans' powers.

A second element in Tsimshian ritual preparation was fasting. Even young children were encouraged to eat lightly occasionally, in order to prepare them for later fasts. Hunters, shamans, warriors, persons preparing for secret society initiations and candidates for hereditary powers also fasted. Girls in seclusion at puberty fasted too; they ended their isolation with a cleansing bath supervised by women relatives. They received no special supernatural favors from the procedure, which was rather regarded as a part of their general training for adult life. The tabus imposed on the pubescent girl were explained as laws laid down by divinities of the myth age.

A third element was body purification, which was usually accomplished by a purgative. A stalk of devil's club chewed, or brewed into a drink, was the most common purgative. An adult's training always involved bathing, fasting and purification, repeated over a period of time. The more dangerous or important the undertaking, the longer the training and the more strictly it was followed.

The contamination of sexual intercourse was abhorrent to supernaturals, hence continence was required of trainees. The continence of hunters was particularly stressed. Wives also observed training tabus, though their schedules of bathing and fasting were not as strict. A wife must be continent while her husband was hunting, lest she destroy the effectiveness of his period of preparation, ruin his luck, or endanger his life. An accident or failure to secure game could, therefore, be blamed on a wife's faithlessness. A menstruant woman's contact with weapons or anything used or touched by the hunter was especially dangerous and undid all his work. Although strict continence on the part of a man who sought a shaman's power or prepared for a secret society initiation is not explicit in the literature, it is implied. The candidate isolated himself from his family, and by implication, from all contaminating influences, and concentrated upon his task.

In the guardian quest, the encounter with a spirit came through a vision, hallucinatory experience, trance or dream. The experience varied from a chance encounter which had slight emotional consequences to highly charged experiences from which the victim never completely recovered. The subject was sometimes described as passing into a coma in which the heart beat and breathing were so imperceptible that observers believed him dead. Others went into a convulsive state resembling epilepsy and frothed at the mouth. Shamans sometimes struggled desperately in this manner with their spirit assailants. The encounter left the initiate exhausted physically and mentally. Only with the assistance of other shamans could he get control of the spirit aides he had received, and thereby avert death. Violent seizures seldom marked the acquisition of power by hunters or warriors, though they were familiar episodes during secret society initiations. However, the initiating spirits of the secret society were called by members and the state of ecstacy or frenzy induced occurred in a carefully planned setting different from that of the seeker in the solitude of the forest.

In the acquisition of hereditary powers, the emotional experience was subordinated to a dramatic presentation. Trances, ecstatic states, and compulsive or other unusual emotional behavior occurred only in the artistic re-enactment of an ancestor's spirit encounter. Some of these performances had lost their original meaning and had become merely the formal showing of a mask or other device, accompanied by music and dance.

A Tsimshian who was under the influence of a spirit was dangerous to non-initiates. He was, therefore, kept apart until it was evident that he was normal again. Recipients of secret society power were dangerous to all who had not been initiated by the same spirits, although these spirits were less menacing to people who had already had many spirit contacts. The initiating spirit was offended by the contamination of the uninitiated, and the latter's life was in jeopardy unless he was also immediately initiated. The initiate was also in danger of punishment by his spirit if he broke any of the tabus imposed during his isolation.

A person who had received power seldom revealed all of the details of his quest or the sources of his aides. A young shaman usually did not reveal the fact that he had had a vision until he felt that his spirit aides were strong enough to compete successfully with those of more experienced practitioners. He then dramatized parts of his experiences, gave euphemistic names to his aides and employed carvings or other devices in demonstrations of his power. These were sometimes magical performances which amazed his audience and contributed to his prestige although unconnected with his curing technique.

Similarly, seekers of power for hunting, acquisition of wealth, and war often waited until they had tested a vision and had achieved success. Then by means of a mask, song, dance or story their experience was made public in a dramatic way, usually at a potlatch.

Inherited Powers and Crests

It is characteristic of Tsimshian mythology that the ancestors met supernaturals while hunting, fishing or traveling, and less often during spirit quests. Most of the spirits were seen by a few men of one lineage. The presence of the same tale in lineages which belonged to different phratries can be explained by the fact that ancestors of several lineages participated in the experience that gave rise to the story. An example is the Nagunaks story claimed by lineages of the Blackfish phratry of the Tsimshian.[3] In this story, ancestors visited the sea monster, who told them that he was also a Blackfish clansman. In the party was one man of an Eagle lineage who also received gifts and the privilege of telling the story of his adventures.

The men who met Nagunaks inadvertently anchored over his house when they were forced to stop for the night. He sent blue cod, one of his slaves, to investigate the cause of the scraping noise on the roof. The steersman was annoyed by the splashing of the fish, caught it and broke its fins. The men then went to sleep and awakened to find themselves and their canoe in a house under the sea. Nagunaks invited the creatures of the sea to a feast at which he instructed the men never to wantonly injure any creature, and he also got promises from the monsters not to harm men in the future. When the feast was over, the men were presented with many gifts and sent home in a copper canoe that flew across the water when struck with a copper paddle. They were surprised to learn that they had been gone four years, for the whole experience had seemed like a dream and they thought they had been away four days. They invited guests, told their story and exhibited the marvelous things they had received. The men of the Blackfish lineage gave one potlatch, and the Eagle clansman with the help of his relatives gave another. The steersman, who was the leader of the fishing party, also received power to approach land and sea animals. He became a successful hunter and very wealthy. Unfortunately, he once took a man hunting with him who disobeyed hunting tabus, and so the power was lost.

Several elements of the guardian spirit quest appear in this story. The men went to sleep and awakened in a strange place. Until the Mouse Woman explained, they did not know what had happened to them, but believed that theirs was a dream or vision experience. They received a magical device by which they reached home, and the leader acquired hunting power. Nagunaks also gave them songs, dances, and new names.

The principal elaboration on this basic guardian spirit quest pattern, developed by the tribes of the northern part of the Northwest Coast area, was in dramatization of the experience, its identification with a lineage, and the use as crests of things the ancestors had heard and seen. The complex of ideas and things became the property of descendants who did not have to go through a supernatural experience again in order to benefit, but needed only to re-enact it by impersonation of the original participants.

Crests derived from the Nagunaks story included the blackfish, a seaweed blanket, copper canoe, and two rooms with carved boards,

[3] Boas, 1916, pp. 285—292; 846 et seq.

These were both symbols of the experience and possessions of the descendants. Representations of the crests, which served as property marks as well as reminders of ancestors' adventures, were carved and painted on ceremonial gear and articles in daily use.

A number of Tsimshian crests were acquired by capturing or killing a monster. For example, Snag-of-the-Sandbar was seen by men from different lineages. They pulled it out far enough to see all the various creatures along its shaft before the tide carried it away. Large Eyes was another monster seen by a man who was starving and, perhaps, out seeking power. He and his relatives pulled it out of the lake, though they had to cut it in half to get it loose. They later gave a feast, adopted it as a crest, and represented it with a large face and no body. Grizzly-Bear-with-Two-Fins was another lake being which was captured and killed. Its skin was given to the discoverer who subsequently had it copied in carvings.[4]

Other powers and crests were acquired by human ancestors or ancestresses who married supernatural beings. One of the most famous was Gauo or Sqawo who was befriended and whose daughter was married by a Sky Being. Their children returned to the mother's village with marvelous powers and weapons which their descendants used, but the latter were not able to duplicate all of the feats of the Sky children.[5]

Tales explaining many crests and powers, which were attributed to remote ancestors of the myth age, have been preserved. Each generation also added new material from the ordinary and marvelous experiences of its members. Thus, each lineage accumulated a rich store of memories preserved in story, song, dance, drama and crests. The supplementations of each successive generation account for the bewildering complexity in crests, powers, names, dances, privileges and prerogatives of the various lineages and also for the diversities in these phenomena among lineages of the same clan.

Furthermore, all experiences which were told about earlier days were cast into the pattern of myth age adventures, and so a separation of myth from historical fact is at best difficult and for the most part impossible. One of the several instances where it is possible to note an historical acquisition of power and crests was recorded by Dr. Barbeau. A party of Gitksan visited the newly built trading post at Bear Lake. "Here they observed the white man, his possessions, and his strange ways, for the first time, and considered their adventure in the nature of a supernatural experience. They were particularly impressed with the white man's dog, the wagon road and the palisade fortification around the houses. They adopted all three as crests, dividing them among the men in the party. They gave two big feasts in the next few years to

[4] Barbeau, 1929, p. 106.
[5] Boas, 1916, pp. 847—850; Barbeau, 1929, p. 80.

which they invited other Gitksan tribes, exhibited their new possessions and adopted them as permanent acquisitions."[6]

Crests and powers were occasionally seized from an enemy people as compensation for Tsimshian relatives who had been killed in battle, or to humiliate the defeated foe. The Tsimshian also seized crests in payment for murder or other crime, but they apparently did not follow the Kwakiutl practice of killing an owner for the sole purpose of acquiring his powers or crests.[7]

Crests sometimes changed hands in compensation for services, upon the extinction of lineages, and as gifts. In the latter case, both the donor and recipient had the right of use. Adoption of foreigners who had prerogatives also accounted for some crests.

Crests and powers were formally assumed at potlatches. The most important of all potlatches celebrated the installation of a house head or tribal chief. He and his relatives re-enacted adventures of ancestors, sometimes impersonating them or the supernaturals they had encountered. The vision or trance was usually portrayed symbolically by means of a dance or carving, or both. The dramatization was treated as a pageant of family history, with emphasis upon the wealth, property, and pride of the lineage of the new chief. Generations of great men were incarnated in the chief, who proudly boasted to his guests that he was foremost of all the tribes, the darling of the supernaturals, and favored by the ancestors. Because of the fact that the tribes of the northern part of the Coast had greater wealth than those of southern Vancouver Island and to the south, they were able to afford more spectacular displays and distributions of wealth. Their emphasis on the cumulative wealth and inherited spirit powers of lineages had resulted in a suppression or displacement of the individual guardian spirit quest.

The Coast Tsimshian and Nisqa initiated very young children into the protective custody of the supernaturals. The throwing dance constituted such an initiation. Each of the invited chiefs who performed this dance sang his song, danced, called upon his power, and indicated its name. Such a name symbolized the guardian spirit acquired by his ancestors and it was used in this fashion only when the spirit was called. The same sort of spirit calling and naming characterized secret society performances. When the power appeared to the chief, he caught it and threw it into the children who were hidden under mats in the corner of the house. Immediately, the whistle belonging to the name began to blow and the children were whisked away by the spirit. After the ceremony, they were ready for secret society initiation or to take part in dramatizations of legends.

[6] Barbeau, 1929, p. 103. This crest was taken after the establishment of Fort St. James in 1808.

[7] Codere, 1950; pp. 102—103 et seq.

At all Tsimshian potlatches which validated a change of status or taking of hereditary rights, names and material from myths were presented in dramatic form. Participants increased their prestige, demonstrated their ability to accumulate wealth, and cited their success as hunters and fishermen. Their ability to give the potlatch demonstrated that the beings of the spiritual world, the guardians of wealth, had assisted them in their worldly efforts.

Secret Societies

The Coast Tsimshian and Nisqa borrowed some secret society names and organization from the northern Kwakiutl, mainly the Heiltsuq and Xaisla.[8] But only two societies, the Dog Eaters and Dancers, gained a firm foothold. The Cannibal, Fire-Thrower and Destroyer dances were acquired as personal, hereditary prerogatives and not as societies.[9] Membership in the Dog Eaters and Dancers was open to any Tsimshian who had the wealth necessary for an initiatory ceremony. House heads sponsored the initiation of sons and daughters and of younger members of their lineages. Novices were coached in every step of the initiation, from the preliminary bathing, fasting and purification to the final removal of spirit influence. The initiation was essentially a planned and formalized guardian spirit quest which was carried out in a public gathering rather than in solitude. The appropriate presiding spirit was called by the songs and symbolized by the dances of the members of the society. The spirit which was in the society dancers seized the novice and he vanished to the accompaniment of whistles. Later, he was heard and seen about the village under the influence of the spirit and without voluntary control over his actions. The state which overcame him corresponded to the vision or hallucinatory experience of a solitary guardian spirit seeker. Society members then enticed the novice, through his spirit, to return to the house where they captured him. His behavior was sometimes so violent that he had to be forcibly restrained. When his ecstacy or frenzy had been brought under control, he danced for his spirit power, and the songs associated with it were sung for him by the society members. Each initiate received an individual dance, song, name and symbol from the tutelary. This parallels the individual and personal manifestation of power received by a solitary seeker.

At Port Simpson, the children of free men, both boys and girls, were initiated into either the Dog Eaters or the Dancers. Persons who belonged to wealthy lineages, or were house heads or their heirs, sponsored further spirit contact experiences in society dances and so increased their prestige, and acquired still stronger power. Only a very wealthy man was able to sponsor as many as four secret society demonstrations.

[8] Boas, 1897a, pp. 632—664.   [9] Garfield, 1939, pp. 293—297.

The Tsimshian did not give up the solitary guardian spirit quest. It, too, was undertaken by seekers of shamanistic powers and by men who desired supernatural assistance in hunting, fishing, warfare and the acquisition of wealth.

In general, the ideology of the supernatural and the associated guardian spirit quest practices had changed to a pattern, one of the primary features of which was the public dramatization of lineage legendary history. A second feature appears in the acquirement of supernatural aides from the lineage ancestry. Direct descendants held prior rights and benefited most from these hereditary privileges. To be sure, the secret society initiations duplicated much of the widespread pattern of the individual guardian spirit quest, but added song composers, dancers, carvers, and other experts. All contacts with the supernatural were determined by hereditary status. Certainly, only persons who had wealth could advance in the ranks of the secret societies. In addition, other secret society dances were acquired from the Kwakiutl as strictly private property so that only one individual in a lineage could come under the influence of a certain supernatural.

Shamanism

Published accounts of Tsimshian shamanism mainly describe shamanistic techniques and give scant information about the sources of shamans' powers or the details of power acquisition.[10] A novice could receive aides from a supernatural who had assisted an ancestor, or from any of the numerous mythical creatures who revealed themselves to human beings. I have been unable to discover evidence that there were certain supernaturals who conveyed shamanistic power only, either by inheritance or otherwise. Shamans appear to have received a particular manifestation from an initiating agent which instructed them to use a curing or other skill in a special way. Some of the tricks such as sleight-of-hand, knife swallowing, and walking on coals, had little direct bearing on professional practice but were as impressive as the shaman's ability to catch a soul and return it to a seemingly dead body.

In Tlingit tales, a candidate was instructed to secure the tongue of a land otter. Possession of the tongue was hazardous because it called the creatures of the unseen world to the seeker. However, it also forced them to convey to him the benefits he sought. If he had observed all the training tabus, he could subdue and control the aides attempting to destroy him so that henceforth they would do his bidding. Employment of a land otter tongue also appears in Tsimshian tales, but as only one of the many agencies through which a shaman received power.

[10] Boas, 1916, pp. 473—477:

A Tsimshian who desired to become a shaman could carry out his own training and quest, though it was more usual for young men to attach themselves to shamans who were paid to teach them. Usually, the young man's maternal uncle, less often his father, paid the pedagogue. Older shamans also took their own sons, nephews or nieces as assistants and supervised their training. The older men sometimes sang their power songs over the novices to help them in their spirit encounters. Experienced shamans also worked with a novice who was in a trance, helped him to get control of the aides he had received, and then revived him.

The following story of acquisition of shamanistic powers was told by a Nass River shaman.[11] It dates from the middle nineteenth century.

When I was a young man I wanted to be a foremost hunter and to be wealthy, so I trained. I was then able to get many animals during the season when their skins were prime and I became wealthy. I saw shamans hunting when the animals were not prime. I tried it and got only poor skins, but the shamans always brought in fine pelts. I was determined to become a shaman also. I told the foremost shaman on Nass River what I wanted and he agreed to train me. He told me to first go to the Bella Bella chief and ask him to give me dancing power.

In the spring I did as the Nisqa shaman directed. The Bella Bella chief agreed to help me after I had given him a gift of many marmot skins. He sent me to Kitga'ata to get power from a shaman there and then to Kitkatla to see two other men who would give me dance powers. He instructed me to go also to Gitando, Gilutsau and Gitwilgoats. He gave me the names of the men to see at each of these places. I was instructed to tell each of them that the Bella Bella chief had agreed to help me.

I went to the villages and each man sang his shaman power songs over me and put further dance powers into me. Then I went home to the Nass, and told the shaman what had happened. He said that I would get power, and instructed me to go to Gitsaxlal where there was a shaman who specialized in making symbols of supernatural power for other shamans.

I told him that I wanted a double-headed, folding knife that I could put into my mouth and it would appear as though I had swallowed it. I gave him presents of marmot skins and he agreed to make it. After many days it was finished. He showed me how to put a bladder of blood in my mouth and then prick it with the knife as I put it in.

I went back to the Nass. That spring I became ill and I was still ill when we moved down to the mouth of the river to fish for olachen. The Nisqa shaman knew that I was now possessed by the powers and he instructed me to call all the shamans who had sung their songs over me. They came and gave me more powers. I had visions in which many aides came to me.

I was now a medicine man and when I got well I gave my performance and showed my symbol of supernatural powers. I was then as famous as the other shamans, and was able to get prime skins at any time of the year.

In this story none of the shamans were chiefs except the man from Bella Bella. Most of the famous Tsimshian shamans were neither lineage

[11] From an account recorded by William Beynon, Port Simpson, British Columbia.

heads nor tribal chiefs. They were men who had achieved distinction and prestige not through hereditary rank but through the use of their special supernatural skills. In potlatches that were given for the transmission of hereditary powers, they participated as lineage members, not as shamans. In the secret society initiations, they again functioned only as members or as individuals who owned dances or privileges. A shaman's sole prerequisite in terms of social position was that he had had experience in controlling spirits.

Witchcraft

The Tsimshian have separate terms for a shaman, who was of course supposed to work for the common good, and for the witch who was literally "an evil person." The witch worked almost entirely through magic. He caused illness or death by enticing or stealing the soul of his victim, or by other means. He might utilize anything intimately associated with the victim's person, such as a nail paring, a bit of clothing or a hair. He put it in a box or wrapped it in a bundle with evil things, said an incantation over it, and hid it. When the contents rotted or the piece of cloth fell from its suspending thread, the victim suffered the illness or misfortune designated by the witch. Shamans were able to diagnose such illness, "see" its cause, and remove it.

The Tsimshian do not seem to have done as much witch hunting as the Tlingit, who were not content until a scapegoat had been found and punished or killed. Tsimshian accounts emphasize the skill of a shaman in counteracting a witch's influence and fighting his powers. Little stress was given to the procedure of torturing a confession out of a person suspected of witchcraft.

CHAPTER FIVE

MYTHOLOGY AND FOLKTALES

The Tsimshian shared many general characteristics of mythology with other tribes of North America and eastern Asia. These similarities included themes, types of plots and specific plots, story characters, episodes and incidents. Among the similarities between eastern Asia and western North America only a few can be included in this brief discussion.

Tales of sky beings, of animals and of supernaturals who conveyed power to humans were widespread. Specific plots included the tale of a girl who married a dog in the guise of a man and bore canine offspring. The liberation of daylight was a widely known plot although Raven in the role of liberator occurred principally on the Northwest Coast. Raven or a comparable culture hero and trickster-transformer was the central character of a series or cycle of tales. Many episodes of the cycle were related on both sides of Bering Sea.

Animal actors or creatures with animal features were very popular. Marriage between humans and animals or animal supernaturals was a dominant theme among Plains tribes as well as on the Northwest Coast and among the Eskimo. Animals or animal supernaturals were usually portrayed as having human attributes. In the greater number of Tlingit and Haida tales, an offended animal married a human being in order to punish or instruct. The animal supernatural spouse in Tsimshian tales most often aided a person in distress and bestowed powers and crests as special gifts.

The mystic relationship between spirit animals and humans was a theme that ran through many tales about animal supernaturals. Animals were killed, or allowed themselves to be killed, to supply food and other benefits to mankind. Rites were performed atoning for the deed and acknowledging man's dependence upon the supernaturals. This theme appeared in many myths of the salmon spirit world and found expression in first salmon rites.

The theme also appeared in many bear tales, including those of girls captured by bears in human guise and of men married to bears who appeared to them as women. Other tales emphasized the bond of friendship between bears and men who obeyed hunters' rites of purification. Rites for the bear were performed in Asia and were present in parts of North America. Although they do not occur as community ceremonials among Northwest Coast tribes, there were individual rites to maintain the relationship between men and bears. Purification of a hunter and sacrifices and prayers to the spirit of the dead animal were essential to success, not only in hunting but in other pursuits.

A long myth about mountain goats who punished a Tsimshian village for wanton killing and disrespectful treatment of their flesh, reflects the same attitude toward sacred spirit animals who must be propitiated to furnish food for mankind.

Trickster stories were particularly popular in the western two-thirds of North America. Raven, Mink and Bluejay were the best known tricksters of the northern part of the Northwest Coast. Coyote was the principal trickster of the southern part of the Northwest Coast, the Southwest, the Plateau and the Plains. Transformer and culture-hero stories were also well known. In many tales of the Tlingit, Haida, northern Kwakiutl and Tsimshian, the traits of transformer, culture-hero and trickster were combined in the principal character. He was usually Raven or a hero identified with him such as the Tsimshian Giant or *Txamsem*. The roles of trickster and transformer were usually separated and ascribed to different characters in tales of the southern Kwakiutl and groups to the south and east of them.

A clear-cut distinction between the events of this world and of other worlds was not usual in North American mythology. The action of a tale or myth often led from this world to an imaginary realm and from everyday events and people to happenings and creatures of the spirit world. Plots, themes and motifs were not of distinctive kinds for myths and tales and many literary components were common to both.[1]

The Tsimshian distinguished between stories of the myth age, and tales, a distinction also made by other Pacific Northwest peoples. The main difference between the two types of narrative was in the setting. The action of myths took place in an age of supernaturals and semi-divine ancestors before the present natural features and social customs of the world were fully established. Tales were set in an essentially modern era in which the action usually occurred in a commonplace setting of hunting, raiding and potlatching, though creatures and happenings of an imaginary realm were also involved.

There were relatively few plots, but there were large numbers of episodes and motifs. There was no close cohesion between episodes and plots. Episodes and motifs moved with considerable freedom from one plot to another and were recombined in many different ways. Some occurred in a large number of different stories, or as separate short stories while others were limited to a few tales or even to a single narrative. Certain themes also recurred in stories that had distinct plots and episode developments. Supernatural aid to despised and distressed human beings and the test theme, both of wide occurrence, were popular

[1] Thompson, 1929.

in Tsimshian folklore. Other Tsimshian themes include mutual aid of brothers, and less often of brothers and sisters, the haughtiness of girls of the upper class, the love of husband and wife, and the affection of uncle and nephew on the one hand and their jealous rivalry on the other. Wealthy chiefs were described much more often than lower class clansmen. Slavery was idealized in descriptions of the love of a slave for his master and his reluctance to be separated from him.

A feature of myths and tales of tribes from southeastern Alaska to the southern part of Vancouver Island which distinguishes this district from adjacent ones was the tendency towards stylistic complexity. The many short, and otherwise unrelated episodes which were told about a celebrated mythical character account for one kind of complexity. Dr. Boas' analysis of the Raven cycle revealed many motifs that occurred elsewhere as separate stories or in other contexts and seem to have become associated with Raven secondarily.[2] Tales of human heroes showed the same kind of elaboration.

Another kind of complexity appeared in the development of the climax. Brothers were vanquished one after another until the youngest succeeded. He then rescued the bodies of the other heroes and brought them back to life. In the Tsimshian myth of *Gauo* she asked, "Who will marry my daughter?" and was answered in turn by stronger and stronger animals whom she rejected. Finally, a stroke of lightning revealed a supernatural Sky Being who helped the women out of their difficulty. Another example is the story of the deserted child who was aided by supernaturals. Each day the supernatural brought food, usually beginning with a few berries or a small piece of fish. Each day larger and larger fish and animals were delivered until whales were left on the beach below the village. These were dried, stored and at length filled all the houses. The starving relatives returned to marvel at the abundance of food and acclaim the deserted man as their chief.

The Tsimshian belief in guardian spirit contact and aid, shared with most North American tribes, ties in with the many supernaturals seen, killed or visited by humans in the tales, as well as with some of the beings described in myths. The belief in marvelous power bestowed by supernaturals also influenced the interpretation of recent events which were incorporated into tales. Several such tolktales describe the emotions of Tsimshian who first saw the white man and his inventions. One of these tales is about fishermen from Kitkatla who were the first of their tribesmen to meet Europeans.[3] Their strange appearance, actions and speech

---

[2] Boas, 1916, pp. 618—641.

[3] From author's field notes. A version appears in Arctander, 1909, pp. 63—65. Capt. James Colnett discovered Nepean Sound in Kitkatla territory in 1787. Captains George Vancouver, in 1791, and Jacinto Caamano, in 1792, visited the Kitkatlas and left some description of them. The story of the first white men seen by the Kitkatlas undoubtedly dates from one of the above visits.

led the Indians to regard them as Ghost People. They were deeply impressed by an iron kettle which, unlike the cooking boxes with which they were familiar, did not burn when set on the fire. The strangers' knives which flashed in the sun seemed to cut magically. A gun and mirror convinced them that they were indeed in the presence of strange and supernaturally potent creatures. The tale shows that the Tsimshian ascribed magical properties to these objects; properties with which they were familiar from long experience with gifts received from supernaturals. The tale is, therefore, an account of the groups' reactions to a new experience and the addition of new crests to the inventory of lineage possessions, cast in familiar literary and ideological form.

Story telling by the Tsimshian was motivated in part by the deep interest of lineages in their history and possessions. Plastic and graphic arts provided symbolically depicted crests, spirit encounters and other events and devices associated with the past. Carvings and paintings were made representing actors in lineage dramas and crests obtained through ancestors' adventures. Such adventures were also dramatized. Oral literature was, therefore, only one aspect of a complex art tradition. It provided themes for carvers, painters and dramatists.

The development of Tsimshian lineages, clans and villages, which was exceedingly complex, was reflected in the oral literature. Many of the fortunes and misfortunes of past generations were preserved in oral traditions which reflect not only actual occurences but also social ideals, customs, and beliefs concerning the former and present world, as Dr. Boas has so competently illustrated in *Tsimshian Mythology*. In spite of its size, this publication is based upon only a fraction of the great numbers of myths, and it is meagerly representative of those tales of the Nisqa and Coast Tsimshian that were identified with separate lineages and clans. The largest available collection of Gitksan myths and tales, only abstracts of which have been published by Dr. Barbeau, explains figures on totem poles.[4]

Most of the Tsimshian literature edited by Dr. Boas, and that collected from the Tlingit and Haida by Dr. Swanton[5] was presented as if it were general community property. Only a few stories in these published collections were identified as the property of or as explanations of historical details of lineages and clans. On the other hand, my own field information demonstrates that certain tales were localized and identified as the property of specific clans or lineages. For example, all Tlingit informants who related the story of *Kats*, the hunter who married the bear woman, agreed that it was the property of the Tlingit *Teqoedi* clan and of certain related Nisqa and Haida lineages. *Kats* was the ancestor

[4] Barbeau, 1929.
[5] Swanton, 1905; 1909.

of these people and the story was told by them as an historical happening, not as a myth, in spite of its content.[6]

All Tlingit and Alaska Haida informants knew at least parts of the Raven cycle of tales. But some of the incidents were regarded as myth accounts of certain lineages of the Raven phratry. Informants who were asked to explain Raven figures on totem poles referred the investigator to the pole owners and asserted that only such individuals knew the versions that had been symbolized on the poles. These stories were almost identical with those recorded by Dr. Swanton and published by him as part of the common literary heritage of all Tlingit. Each such story told to me was localized in the area that belonged to the lineage of the pole owner, or a lineage ancestor was alleged to have been present when the incident took place. Stories told to account for pole carvings included the bringing of daylight, Raven's loss of his beak to the halibut fishermen, Raven's journey in the whale, and his marriage to Fog Woman who made the first salmon. Raven's journey to the Sky where he married Sun's daughters was also illustrated on lineage-owned Tlingit poles. This story was prefaced with the Deluge myth. Raven's journey beneath the sea was also illustrated in carving. As a result of this adventure, he taught the ancestors to utilize sea mammals and shellfish for food.

It is important to note that versions of these stories were told as privately owned lineage legends and were regarded as different stories from the same incidents when they were included in the general Raven cycle related by Tlingit and Haida story tellers.

The collections of Tlingit, Haida and Tsimshian folklore analyzed by Dr. Boas in *Tsimshian Mythology* led him to conclude that "There is no connection whatever between the Raven myth and the social grouping of the people, except the vague statement, that is not found embodied in any version as an important element, that Raven was the ancestor of the Raven Clan. This idea is certainly foreign to the Tsimshian. There is no mention whatever in the Raven myth of the ancestors of any of the local subdivisions of the exogamic groups."[7] Although carvings of Raven appeared on Tsimshian totem poles studied by Dr. Barbeau, he asserts that there were no particular tales to account for these other than the general Raven myth.[8] On the other hand, the Gitksan carvings of Raven described by Dr. Barbeau did not illustrate any incidents from the Raven cycle of tales as recorded in *Tsimshian Mythology*.

The identification of Raven tales with ancestors of certain lineages by the Tlingit and Haida may be unique and recent. However, further

[6] Garfield and Forrest, 1949, pp. 30—33.
[7] Boas, 1916, p. 619. The same can be said for a number of other tales which, however, the Indians know are the property of certain lineages.
[8] Barbeau, 1929, p. 50.

collection of myths and tales should be undertaken with particular attention to those regarded as part of the common heritage of everyone, distinct from those that belong to specific lineages. Such a study would reveal the extent to which myth elements, known over wide areas, were reworked into clan and lineage "histories."

Myths of the Tsimshian, as well as those of the Tlingit and Haida, do give evidence of literary reworking of separate tales of the Raven cycle into the semblance of a life history of the culture hero. The cycle begins with Raven's birth, either as the child of a faithless woman or as the unwanted nephew of a jealous uncle. The uncle is frequently identified as the powerful supernatural being who controlled the sky and the earth and oceans beneath. It was he who ordained that Raven should become the culture hero, bringing benefits to man. He did not give up his powers without a contest since Raven must prove himself worthy of the task. The cycle proceeds with the acquisition of supernatural power by Raven, either through a contest with his uncle or through heavenly birth or rebirth. He then returned from the sky where he was born or to which he ascended to escape a world covered with water. Here a synthesis of the Deluge myth and Raven story has been made which correlates the beginning of his life and activities with the emergence of the modern world. In several versions, his first significant act was to make the waters subside.

The insatiable appetite of the transformer is one of the most characteristic and widespread themes of the Raven cycle as told in Northwest America. The Tlingit, Haida and Tsimshian attempted to account for this characteristic. In most versions, the supernatural one, who did not eat, was fed scabs. His transformation into a creature with human appetite was overdone and he became voracious. This episode gives meaning to his subsequent behavior.[9]

The separate Tsimshian stories are linked by literary devices which carry Raven from one place and adventure to another. The arrangement of incidents, beginning with the circumstances of Raven's birth, contrasts tales of frustration, voraciousness and outright trickery with those of an awakening social responsibility and ends on the motif of the culture hero voluntarily divested of his trickster role. In the final episode, Raven invited dangerous sea monsters to a feast and turned them into stone so that they could no longer harm human beings. He then transformed himself and his carved house to stone.

Raven tales from the Tlingit and Haida show that narrators had the same feeling for a logical and traditional sequence of incidents though failing memories and lack of agreement among raconteurs have left us with cycles pieced together from separately told tales by different narrators. The Tlingit, Haida and Tsimshian share most motifs and

[9] Boas, 1902; 1916, pp. 638—641.

agree on the order of some of the stories. Several stories have not been reported from any other groups. One of these is the short account of the origin of death as the result of Elderberry giving birth before Stone. Raven decreed that human beings would be as enduring as stone if she gave birth first. Another is the account of the origin of tides by pulling the Tide Woman from the cave and the consequent release of the tide line. The origin of salmon from the Fog Woman whom Raven married and offended has been reported only from the above three groups and their immediate neighbors.

The Raven cycle and many of the separate stories included in it are widespread in western America and Asia.[10] Comparison of these leads to the conclusion that the Tsimshian, Haida and Tlingit achieved a degree of integration and cohesion of the tales not found elsewhere. They added independent motifs and stories to the cycle and invented new ones, including an introduction accounting for Raven's birth and presence on the earth. These they wove into the semblance of a unified epic by arrangement of incidents, by supplying motivation for actions and by means of the concluding story of his transformation.

Analysis of similarities between Tsimshian oral literature and that of their neighbors reveals the closest affinities with the Tlingit and Haida. The Tsimshian share many stories with the Western Plateau, as well as plots, themes and independent motifs that are woven into dissimilar tales. They share fewer characteristics with coastal tribes to the south of them.

[10] Jochelson, 1905; Hatt, 1949.

CHAPTER SIX

The Arts

Drama, Dancing and Music

The Tsimshian were able musicians, dancers and dramatists. Ancient legends, visitations of tutelary spirits, and current happenings were reenacted for the glorification of chiefs and their lineages, for the spiritual benefit of individuals and for the pleasure and instruction of spectators. Dancing and music were inseparable parts of the unfolding dramatic scene, accomplished as much through the medium of symbolic dancing as through acting. The dramatic impact of the performance was heightened by the use of costumes and masks, of painted screens and of mechanical devices such as dancing heads and spouting whales. Performers were accompanied by choruses of women singers and one or more drummers. Artists, song composers, dance instructors and directors combined their talents in preparing and staging performances.

Instrumental music was limited to a few rhythm-producing instruments. The Coast Tsimshian and Nisqa used a large box drum and wooden rattles (see Pl. 1) as the principal accompaniment to songs and dances. The Gitksan probably also used the tambourine type of drum, known to their Athapascan neighbors. Wooden whistles were used as the voices or calls of secret society tutelary spirits but did not serve as musical instruments.

In contrast to the paucity of musical instruments, Northwest Coast tribes had a wealth of songs for every occasion. Songs were among the treasured gifts from supernatural beings and were handed down with the legends and crests gained by lineage ancestors. Songs were also revealed or given by tutelary spirits of the secret societies and these were also treasured by their owners. Nearly every clan legend includes at least one song composed to commemorate an ancestor or some event in his career. The most sacred were hymns sung only in times of bereavement or great stress. Other, less sacred songs belonging to lineage members included nursery songs which often referred to ancestors' pecularities or doings, songs relating to crests, disasters and victories. Still others, both traditional and new, were common property.

The Tsimshian honored the talented composer who could supply new songs for feasts, potlatches and secret society initiations. A host, planning an affair, engaged the services of a composer to arrange melodies and words, and teach them to his group. This was done in secret so that guests did not know in advance what they were to hear. The host requested songs of praise for his achievements and the glorification of his ancestors. But even more, he desired cleverly worded comments on the weaknesses and defections of selected guests. These derisive songs did not openly insult guests since that was neither polite nor safe. Oblique and subtle references, plays on words and the use of words with double meaning evoked admiration from the audience and left little doubt of the identity of the intended victims. The words of such songs are extremely difficult to translate into intelligible English without copious footnotes, but a number have been recorded for the Tsimshian, Haida, Tlingit and Fort Rupert Kwakiutl. Dr. Swanton states that Haida songs of derision were largely in Tsimshian which the Haida could not translate.[1] This suggests that humiliation of a rival in song was a recent borrowing from Tsimshian.

Song contests between rivals or as means of settling quarrels are known from the Alaska Eskimo, the Aleutian Islands and possibly from Kamchatka.[2] Usually two individuals composed and sang derisive songs at each other until the audience declared one the winner. Northwest Coast battles with song were not so direct but were also waged according to formal rules. A victim could not retaliate until he was host at a feast or potlatch. He then composed his own insults or engaged the services of a talented song maker. Eskimo and Northwest Coast song contests are analogous and undoubtedly are historically related.

So much has been written about Northwest Coast dramatic performances that a brief summary will suffice here. The Tsimshian reenacted episodes from clan legends at all public events but especially at the funeral services of a chief and the installation ceremony of his successor. They also presented skits depicting humorous situations, narrow escapes or serious events of everyday life with skill and a lively sense of mimicry. The Coast Tsimshian did imitations of interior Athapascan manners, speech and dress for the amusement of guests. In later years, they added burlesques of Russians, Americans, Englishmen and even Aleuts and Japanese to their repertory.

The Coast Tsimshian acquired two secret societies and many individual spirit dances from their northern Kwakiutl neighbors, together with the rich pageantry required for initiation of novices and demonstrations of powers. These in turn were passed on to the Nisqa and southern Gitksan through marriage and purchase, though the Gitksan also acquired dance prerogatives directly from the Kitimat. Potlatching and secret society activities were never so important to the northern Gitksan, hence their dramatic performances were neither so numerous nor so elaborate as those of the rest of the Tsimshian.

[1] Swanton and Boas, 1912, p. 63.
[2] Birket-Smith and de Laguna, 1938, p. 464.

The area of elaborate presentation of dramatic performances includes the Tlingit, Haida, Tsimshian, Kwakiutl, Bella Coola and Nootka. The number and complexity of performances fade out rapidly from this center of Northwest Coast theatrical art.

Painting, Engraving and Sculpture

The distinctive plastic and graphic arts of the Northwest Coast were produced by tribes from the Gulf of Georgia to Yakutat Bay. It was in this area that concepts of hereditary status and wealth held sway and where potlatch and secret society performances provided ample opportunity for skill in the making of decorated articles. The most elaborate work was done by the Haida, Tlingit and Tsimshian whose complex clan organization stimulated artistic production, and by the northern Kwakiutl, whose secret society dramatizations provided inspiration for creative artists. Excellent work was also done by southern Kwakiutl, Bella Bella, Bella Coola and Nootka carvers.

As craftsmen familiar with carpentry tools and woodworking techniques, men were also the carvers, painters and sculptors. In addition to wood, they worked in bone, stone, horn and copper, shaping and ornamenting all materials with equal skill, though by far the most work was done in wood. Their artistic talents were not confined to articles to be used only on rare public occasions but were also applied to the fashioning and ornamentation of implements and household furnishings in daily use. Proportionately as much time, thought and skill were lavished on these homely articles as on more venerated and spectacular masks, memorial columns or housefront paintings.

Wooden chests, serving dishes and trays, cooking and storage boxes, spoons, fish hooks and clubs, and canoes were manufactured and ornamented for daily use. Handsomely made horn spoons and the more lavishly decorated chests and dishes were reserved for feast use and for gifts. Ornaments of bone and copper were worn by both men and women.

Equipment reserved for special occasions included carved and painted rattles, drums, headdresses and masks. Ornamented chests held the remains of the dead, and carved and painted columns were raised in memory of the deceased. The most spectacular products were the paintings which covered the facades of houses and the timbers carved with symbolic figures, generally known as totem poles. Facade paintings seem to have been more popular with the Coast Tsimshian who made few carved columns compared to the numbers in Gitksan and Nisqa villages.[3] In this they resemble the Kwakiutl and more southerly tribes.

Much of the subject matter of Northwest Coast art was drawn from legendary history, quasi-historic events and myths of the world's be-

[3] Barbeau, 1929, pp. 14—15; Boas, 1916.

ginnings. Historic experiences were related as myths or tales in which ancestors, spiritual and human, participated. Some legends dealt with origins of present day customs and lineages. Many tales were identified with the forebears and history of particular lineages. Incidents and actors from such tales were the source of designs used to decorate articles of everyday as well as ceremonial use. Totems and crests of kinship groups were derived from all the above sources.

The predominant actors in myths and tales were supernatural beings or human-like spirits, who in both instances had animal characteristics. Other actors were semi-historical ancestors whose contact with the supernatural world had endowed them with spiritual qualities. The intense pre-occupation of the Tsimshian and their neighbors with legendary history of lineages and spirit contacts of ancestors and the need to develop tangible means of preserving ancestors' experiences were primary factors in the development of the arts of painting, engraving and sculpture. The goal of the artist who worked in plastic and graphic forms was to illustrate actors and incidents so that they would be readily recognized by observers familiar with the tales. The art was not essentially a vehicle for the recording of events and people of everyday life. Living or recently deceased people were seldom depicted. If they were, it was usually because they had been through spiritual experiences which they or their relatives wished to commemorate.

Human and animal-supernatural heroes challenged the ingenuity and skill of the artist. Myth characters were transformed into animals, men, birds or inanimate objects, sometimes within the action of a single tale. The number of story heroes or dominant characters was limited and there was a tendency to weave many plots and incidents about a single hero. In the well-known and widely told Raven tales there is only one notable hero who is an actor with many-sided personality. Carvers and painters developed a set of symbols by which the people recognized the various characters, incidents and plots that were represented. Illustrations of a few popular subjects became so conventionalized that carvings or paintings of them are readily recognizable whether they come from Yakutat or Vancouver Island. On the other hand, illustrations representing individual experiences could not be interpreted, even by a tribesman, without explanation from the owner or artist.

In the process of graphic conventionalization, distinctive features of each oft-recurring story character were selected.[4] The shape of the beak was the distinguishing mark of birds and of bird supernaturals. Characteristic fin and tail shapes identified sea mammals and fish. Head and tail differences established the identity of land animals or of animal supernaturals. Since many myth heroes were human-like spirits, illustra-

[4] Boas, 1927, pp. 183—298. Also see illustrations of Tsimshian wood carving and painting.

tions often combined human limbs and bodies with animal symbols. Ordinary human beings were provided with human shaped ears, facial features and bodies. Inanimate objects and sky and earth phenomena were also represented. There was no attempt to include all the story characters in a single carving or painting.

The development of the art style was influenced by several factors in addition to subject matter as such. The material employed influenced the development of the style. Artists painted and carved soft wood and sculptured stone and bone. They also painted on wood and on hides. They decorated surfaces as large as the front of a house and as small as the face of a bone charm. They sculptured tiny ear ornaments or sixty-foot totem poles with equal skill. Much of the artistic energy was expended upon houses, canoes, clothing, storage chests, serving dishes and other articles where the ornamentation was not allowed to interfere with utility.

Certain principles guided the artist in the formal treatment of a decorative field and in the arrangement of design upon surfaces of varying sizes and shapes. The design usually covered all or nearly all of the decorative field. Identifying marks or symbols of the subject must be included. They were often exaggerated in size in relation to the rest of the body, which if possible must also be included. Subjects were more often represented in front view, less often in profile or from the top looking down on the back of the subject.

There were three main principles of representation: the conventional details of the subject must be emphasized; the whole must be represented, not merely a part of the whole; and the design must conform to the shape of the surface to be decorated. From the point of view of realistic representation, these principles resulted in extensive distortion. The subject was dissected or split and spread out, though the relationship of body parts was usually preserved. However, the subject was sometimes dismembered and the body parts represented were so highly stylized as to be virtually unrecognizable (see Fig. 2).

Although a very limited number of basic design elements were used by Northwest Coast artists the combinations of these elements produced a bewildering variety of effects (see Fig. 3). Curved lines and rounded angles were characteristic of all design elements. The basic form was a rectangle with rounded corners; one end was slightly wider than the other. The base line was often curved. True circles were used less frequently than ovals or rectangles, which were used to represent eyes, faces, and joints and as non-significant formal elements to fill in the background around a central figure. Another basic element that appeared in every design was the so-called feather tip; often it was asymmetrical in outline or in the balance of fill-in lines. This element represented bird feathers, fish and sea mammal fins and tails, ears and limbs of animals

Figure 2. Design on the Side of a Wooden Box
(after Boas, drawn by Steven Dunthorne).

and supernaturals, cheek outlines, and teeth. It appeared extensively as a part of formal designs to fill in background spaces. Two other frequently used elements were the crescent and an element often of claw-like shape based on the triangle. Connecting lines of tapering widths served to outline figures and to tie the parts of a design into a compact and recognizable whole.

Figure 3. Abstract Design from Side of Box
(After Boas, drawn by Steven Dunthorne).

Designs on flat surfaces were generally more highly stylized than designs of other kinds. In sculpture, either in the round or in relief, the artist approached realism, the degree of realistic representation depending on the purpose for which the carving was made. Startlingly life-like masks, heads and figurines prove that artists were capable of producing such effects. Even in sculpture which was essentially conventionalized, some creatures were illustrated in more realistic form than others. For example, frogs were almost always sculptured without resort to conventionalization. Halibut, salmon, whales and blackfish were also frequently accorded realistic representation. Small dishes, especially those for serving grease, were frequently carved out in animal shapes that are more readily recognizable than the representations of these animals on flat surfaces.

Artists painted and carved designs, either independently or in combination. They sculptured both in the round and in relief. Decorated flat surfaces included square or rectangular sides of drums and chests, dish ends, and house fronts and partitions. Curved surfaces included bowls of spoons, sides of dishes, and canoes. Sculptured objects included house posts, mortuary columns and figures, totem poles, spoon handles, masks, rattles, and halibut hooks. Each surface shape and contour presented special problems. There were two methods of approach: one appropriate to the decoration of flat surfaces, the other to sculpture of blocks of wood or stone. But the two were not mutually exclusive. Details on sculptured figures, such as the wings of birds, were often treated, whether by carving or painting, in the same manner as designs applied to flat surfaces. Combinations of painted, carved and sculptured elements appeared on all types of wood articles. Those of bone and stone were seldom painted.

If paint was applied to carved and sculptured designs, it was used only to emphasize details such as eyes, eyebrows, teeth, wing elements and claws. True paintings were made on natural wood or dressed skins, and occasionally on baskets, mats and woven hats. There was no shading of colors. Each color was a flat, solid design element distinctly set off from another element by black lines or by the natural color of the background. Pigments were few. The most abundant and easily procured was ochre. It produced colors of dull yellow, brown, orange-red and bright red according to the per cent of iron oxide in relation to other minerals or impurities, and according to the method used in its preparation. Lumps of ochre were wrapped in cedar bark and baked to produce brown and dark red, the shade depending partly on the heat and partly on the length of time of baking. Black was secured mainly from graphite and manganese. White, which was seldom used by the Tsimshian, was made from shells burned in the fire. A rare and highly prized blue-green pigment was made from copper-impregnated clays obtained in trade from tribes that lived in copper-bearing areas. Pigments were ground in stone mortars and mixed with salmon eggs chewed to a smooth paste. The resulting paint had a rich heavy texture, good coverage and a slight gloss. It was as durable as good commercial paints. Brushes were made of bristles, hairs, and vegetable fibers fastened to wooden or bone handles that often were carved. Brushes were cut diagonally and did not taper to a point or have straight edges. Like other tools, brushes were drawn toward the artist when painting.[5]

Metal Work

Copper was worked in pre-European times in wide areas of North America. In the Northwest, cold hammering was known from Cook Inlet inland to the Mackenzie River and south in the Plateau area to the Nez Perce. Copper working on the coast extended to the Nootka of southern Vancouver Island. It is also reported for the Chinook at the mouth of the Columbia River in Washington.[6] Surface ores were utilized and no attempt was made to mine or smelt ores. Cold hammering, cutting and riveting were the only techniques of fabrication, though the latter may date from eighteenth century European contact.

[5] Niblack, 1890, p. 282, Pl. XLV, a and b.
[6] Birket-Smith and de Laguna, 1938, pp. 404—405; Rickard, 1939.

Copper was employed for arrow heads, daggers and ornaments, and for inlay in wood and horn. Beaten shields in which wealthy men invested large amounts of property were also fashioned. Because of its malleability and resistance to disintegration it was used over and over and was re-manufactured into new articles as fashions or demands changed. Pieces were also pounded or riveted together to make larger articles or they were cut into smaller ones.

Use of copper is archaeologically recent but definitely pre-European on the Northwest Coast. There is sufficient testimony of eighteenth century traders and explorers to establish the fact that the Tlingit, Haida and Nootka, with whom traders made their first contacts, were thoroughly familiar with the metal, manufactured it into objects of typical Northwest Coast designs and traded them and the raw ores widely. There is no certain reference in eighteenth century accounts to Tsimshian copper work, but there is little doubt that they were then also familiar with copper. They do not seem to have had as much of it as the Tlingit and Haida who were closer to the main supplies. When and where copper working was first introduced into Northwest America are questions which cannot be answered without further study.

For the Northwest Coast tribes, the principal source of native copper was the Copper River basin in Athapascan territory. The main middlemen were the northern Tlingit, who either manufactured it for trade or bartered the raw lumps of ore. The Tsimshian procured small amounts of ore from surface deposits on Peace and Nass Rivers and from the Cassiar district. Other sources were the Queen Charlotte Islands and Hetta Inlet on Prince of Wales Island. It is also possible that some copper reached the northern Tsimshian from Coppermine River in the Arctic.

Fur traders report that the Indians displayed great interest in the work of craftsmen aboard their vessels and that copper and iron were in great demand.[7] Both metals were reworked by native craftsmen into articles of their own design. They also learned to work gold and silver into ornaments, combining traditional designs and methods of workmanship with those learned from the newcomers.[8]

By the latter part of the nineteenth century silver largely replaced copper for ornaments. At the present time, native handicrafts in metals have largely ceased in favor of commercially produced and store-purchased jewelry.

Eighteenth century visitors found Northwest Coast Indians in possession of iron daggers, knives and ornaments. Within a short time,

[7] Joyce Wike Holder has collected data on trade goods, especially copper and iron, brought to the Northwest Coast by maritime fur traders. There were marked changes in native preferences from year to year (mss.).

[8] Quimby (1948) lists Chinese and Hawaiian artisans on vessels visiting the Northwest Coast between 1785 and 1795.

probably no more than a year or two after the first trading vessels arrived, hatchets, iron pots and knives were spread throughout most of the trading area.

According to Tsimshian tradition, halibut fishermen from the village of Kitkatla were the first Tsimshian to acquire iron articles. One fisherman received a hatchet and another an iron pot from men who came in a sailing vessel. Other coastal Tsimshian acquired iron from Haida and Tlingit fur hunters during the last decade of the eighteenth century. At about the same time, or a few years later, the Tsimshian were obtaining iron from tribes in contact with mainland trading posts.

Weaving and Clothing

The outstanding contribution of women artists to the distinctive arts of the Northwest Coast is the woven blanket. Tsimshian women have been given credit for originating the famous Chilkat robe, woven of yarn made of twisted mountain-goat wool and fibers of yellow cedar bark. A robe woven of twisted cedar bark was the prototype of the Chilkat blanket. Blankets of cedar bark alone or of a combination of bark and dog hair, mountain-goat wool or pulled feathers were made by some of the coastal tribes from Puget Sound to Chilkat River, and by a few tribes of the interior of Washington and British Columbia. Some were woven with an unornamented background in twilled diagonal weave with a border of three-stranded twist weave. Others were bordered with zigzag colored lines. Still others had horizontal or diagonal bands of geometric designs woven into the body of the blanket and were without borders.[9]

The Chilkat robe is characterized by conventionalized designs derived from those developed by men for the decoration of wooden articles. The men painted pattern boards for the weavers to follow. The designs are entirely different from the geometric decorations used by the women on mats and baskets, and on the older rectangular blankets. Also characteristic of the Chilkat robe is the method of joining design elements to the background with loop stitches. The warp yarn was a double strand of twisted cedar bark covered with mountain-goat wool, doubled and twisted a second time so that the bark cord was concealed. The woof was of mountain-goat wool. Colors were black, yellow and blue-green patterns on a background of natural white wool.

Chilkat designs were usually arranged in three fields, similar to the layout of designs on other flat surfaces. A wide center field covered the back of the wearer. There was a narrower strip on each side which extended over the shoulders and was visible from the front. This was similar to the arrangement of painted designs on the front edges of skin

[9] Emmons, 1903.

robes. A wide fringe finished the sides and bottom, and a narrow band of fur was often used to trip the top edge. Robes, shirts, aprons and leggings were made on the simple upright loom known to all Northwest Coast weavers.

By the beginning of the twentieth century, the Tsimshian had forgotten the art of blanket weaving. Only the Chilkat Tlingit among all northwestern coastal peoples were continuing to make blankets. By 1930, only a very few of the older women remembered the technique. In an effort to revive the art, the Arts and Crafts Board of the Office of Indian Affairs employed these women to teach younger women.

Chilkat robes were heirlooms of wealthy families, worn only on special occasions. There are many references in the literature to these robes and to the headgear and ornaments worn with them. Leggings and an apron reaching almost to the knee were also a part of the costume. These were woven or of dressed skin, ornamented with fringes and bands of fur. Quill embroidery or painted designs were also used on skin garments. Colorful and elaborate, these nineteenth century ceremonial costumes are well known. There is very little information concerning Tsimshian everyday clothing of the late eighteenth and early nineteenth centuries. Furs and dressed skins were bartered to traders for blankets, cloth and garments which replaced native clothing.

Before the introduction of manufactured clothing Coast Tsimshian and Nisqa men and women wore small skin aprons fastened front and back to a belt. No trousers or shirts were worn. Robes or blankets of cedar bark, fur and dressed skins were worn for warmth and to shed rain. Poor people wore marmot pelts while marten, seal and sea otter were worn by the wealthy.[10] Elk, moose and groundhog skins were important barter items but there are no descriptions of their use as clothing. Moccasins were not regularly worn on the coast.

The Tsimshian of the interior wore dressed skin clothing, fur robes and moccasins. Their shirts, leggings and women's robes fastened with ties, and partially fitted. They were decorated with fringes, paint and quill embroidery. Further details are lacking.

Tsimshian shamans wore fringed dancing aprons of dressed skin and carried their paraphernalia in skin bags. Bear skin robes were also worn by some shamans. Bear claw crowns and necklaces of carved animal figures were part of a shaman's working costume and are the only items of apparel mentioned for female shamans.[11]

Skin dressing, sewing and quill embroidery were women's skills. They also wove hats, baskets and matting of cedar bark, spruce root and other vegetable fibers. Conical, wide brimmed hats were worn by both men and women. Tlingit and Haida women decorated their expertly made

[10] Boas, 1916, p. 52.
[11] *Ibid.*, p. 558.

spruce root hats and baskets with imbricated geometric designs in colored grasses and maiden hair fern stems. Their workmanship is superior to that of Tsimshian women, whose cedar bark baskets were coarse and often unornamented. Fine baskets to be used as potlatch gifts and hats for ceremonial wear were usually obtained from the Haida.

Most Tsimshian masks were of one piece without movable parts. They also made a distinctive chief's headdress. A rectangular wooden placque, carved with crest figures and bordered with shell inlay was attached to a headband and worn like a crown. Weasel skins hung down the back and flicker feathers and sea-lion bristles stood upright around the headband.

Polished bone charms carved into low relief animal and bird figures were also made by the Tsimshian, and less frequently by other tribes.

The Development of Representational Art

The focal area of development of Northwest Coast representative art is within the boundaries of Nisqa, Coast Tsimshian, southern Tlingit and Haida territory. It is impossible to assign the honor of spearheading the development to any one group. Artists of each group made contributions and received stimulus from others. Artisans and artists were frequently commissioned from distant villages to make canoes or carve poles on order. Decorated articles also changed hands in the extensive barter between tribes and as gifts in potlatches. Thus, there were constant interchanges of ideas among men receptive to innovation.

Columnar carvings were made by the Coast Tsimshian and Nisqa before the Gitksan took over that form of illustrating myths and lineage histories. House pillars and short memorial posts antedated the tall, free standing columns decorated with four or more large figures, generally called totem poles. Crest paintings on the fronts of houses were also made by the Tsimshian before totem poles became popular.

Tsimshian style of carving and arrangement of figures on totem poles were more closely allied to Tlingit work than to that of the Haida. Figures on Tsimshian and Tlingit poles were often separated from each other and stood, squatted or sat in relaxed postures. Blocked-out masses were large and simple, uncomplicated by small, interlocking figures or the engraved detail prevalent in Haida work. Postures of succeeding figures were often similar, repeating masses and curves the length of the timber. Mask-like faces on Tsimshian poles were frequently detached from bodies, a stylistic feature not often found on Haida and Tlingit columns. Tsimshian carvers seldom separated the head from the body by a columnar neck and sloping shoulders as was often done by the Tlingit. However, a small tab ear with a simple engraved chevron-shaped inner ear is characteristic of Tlingit and Tsimshian carving, and distinct from that of the Haida.

Tlingit and Tsimshian carvings also resemble each other in the combinations of static and animated figures, especially those surmounting a pole. Birds and animals in high relief and in the round appear to climb or to be in flight. Figures on Haida poles were usually compact and static, though there are a few notable exceptions.

Elaborately fashioned bird rattles were also of Tsimshian origin. Small figures of men, frogs and faces representing the placques on chiefs' headdresses were usually carved on the tops of these rattles.

Questions concerning dating of Northwest Coast representative art as expressed in painting, engraving and sculpture can only be answered in general terms in this brief discussion. However, enough documentary and archaeological evidence has been accumulated to conclusively establish a pre-maritime fur trade date for the full development of the representative style of decoration in the media of wood, stone, bone and copper.

A number of students have combed writings and drawings of explorers and maritime fur traders for references to decorated articles which the latter saw and bartered from the Indians.[12] They demonstrate conclusively that the distinctive characteristics of design known from the extensive collections and literature of the nineteenth century, were in existence before the middle of the eighteenth century. A wide variety of ornamented articles was seen and described by explorers and traders, showing that native craftsmen with long experience had applied their skill to many forms and materials. They were not beginners timorously experimenting, but trained and talented virtuosos capable of realizing the full potentialities of their media within the limits of their artistic traditions.

Archaeological evidence of Northwest Coast art work is, and will probably remain, meager. Non-perishable materials were not used nearly as extensively as wood which deteriorates rapidly. Also, no satisfactory system of dating for pre-European sites has been devised. Stone and bone engravings and sculpture have been found but their precise dates are not known. The situation is complicated by the fact that designs in stone are sometimes geometric or crude animal figures only faintly resembling those done in wood. Whether the styles of ornamentation represent differences in age, in purpose or in techniques of working materials is not yet clear.

Representative art on the Northwest Coast was thoroughly integrated with mythology, kinship structure and function, and with concepts of hereditary wealth in all their ramifications. Such thoroughgoing consistency was the result of a long process of dynamic growth within the area and could not have occurred in a few decades or a few generations, nor as the result of recent diffusion of whole complexes.

[12] Newcombe, 1931, pp. 8—9; Keithahn, 1945, pp. 21—33; Barbeau, 1929, pp. 192—209; Drucker, 1948; Paalen, 1943, pp. 7—17.

This conclusion does not rule out the importance of comparative analyses of Pacific Rim cultural elements, and detailed study of the origin and diffusion of elements. Neither does it deny that better understanding of the local developments may be gained by setting the Northwest Coast against the background of a much broader area. One example will suffice. Carved columns, raised as grave markers or in memory of a deceased person are, of course, widespread. Wooden columns carved with a human or animal figure are known from the Eskimo of the lower Yukon and southward, from Athapascan tribes in Alaska and British Columbia and from tribes of the Washington littoral.[13] Carved grave markers were made by the Ainu and carved or painted posts occur in eastern Siberia.[14] Short posts on which personal possessions were hung were raised in the same area and also by Alaska Eskimo and many northern Athapascans. Most of the carved grave markers or memorial posts were short, plain shafts surmounted by one or two rudely fashioned figures representing the family connections of the deceased or some major event in his career. However, it is a far cry from the simple post in an Ainu or lower Yukon River graveyard to the elaborate memorial columns and totem poles in a Tsimshian or Haida town, not only in the styles of carving but especially in the cultural milieu to which each belongs. In such a comparison, the unique and localized features of Northwest Coast art stand out in definite contrast.

The opening of the era of exploration and maritime fur trading in the middle of the eighteenth century especially favored those Northwest Coast tribes living along the migration routes of the seal and sea otter. During the thirty to forty years before the animals were virtually annihilated, the coast Indians supplied the majority of pelts and acted as middlemen between their less strategically located countrymen and the traders.

The maritime fur traders scarcely interferred with the Indians' way of life but offered them new riches and, in many instances, more efficient implements and techniques. The quantity of iron received in barter met their tool needs within a few years. While most of the metal was reworked into native types of tools, the Indians also adopted European axes to fell trees and dress timbers, and chisels to improve detail carving. They developed more efficient methods of moving and raising timbers, and reduced the labor of house building and pole raising. In addition, they received quantities of trade goods far beyond their former ability to accumulate. Production in all the traditional decorative arts was increased and new arts, such as silver work and pipe making were added. Part of the new wealth was invested in totem poles which were only

---

[13] Newcombe, 1931, p. 8; Nelson, 1899, pp. 317—319, Fig. 104; Krieger, 1927, Pls. 3 and 15; Barnett, 1942.
[14] Jochelson, 1924, P. 13, Fig. 2; Kindaiti, 1941, pp. 44—47.

further developments of columnar carvings which previously had appeared principally on house and mortuary posts. The totem pole, as distinct from mortuary and house-post carvings, was, therefore, an achievement of the fur trade era.

The new wealth also increased the number and lavishness of potlatches, secret society and hereditary power demonstrations, feasts and entertainment. These in turn intensified the demand for masks, headdresses and other paraphernalia, and contributed to greater specialization among artists and craftsmen.

Traders and explorers collected many decorated articles of native manufacture and so augmented local demands for art work, though the most extensive museum and private collections were made during the nineteenth century. Native craftsmen were influenced from the first contacts by European, Asiatic and Pacific Island artisans whom they observed, and by the preferences of the foreigners for certain trade articles over others. Models of carved poles, canoes, and chests were readily taken by the visitors. Foreign objects, such as pipes were also copied and decorated according to traditional principles of perspective, line drawing and subject matter, combined with those learned from the foreigners.

The Nootka, the Haida and the Tlingit of Sitka were the first Northwest Coast tribes to come in contact with fur traders. They were also the earliest middlemen who bartered foreign goods to less fortunately situated neighbors in exchange for furs. Access to fur-bearing land animals was the principal advantage enjoyed by tribes of the mainland, including the Tsimshian.

During this period art work flourished. Carvers developed individual styles, introduced new designs and trained younger men. Their services and the things they made were in demand in distant villages and decorative arts diffused. Thus, totem-pole making spread from the Nass into Gitksan territory, and Nisqa carvers were hired to fashion poles and train local men.

The take of sea otter and fur seal had seriously declined by 1825 and a few years later these animals were almost extinct. Fur traders then turned to land animals which were not so valuable. European trappers also invaded the country and economic prosperity, so far as the Indians were concerned, was over. The first serious smallpox epidemic took its toll in the 1830's. By 1880, prospectors, trappers, traders and settlers were coming in in increasing numbers, and with them came diseases which further depleted Indian villages. The native cultural heritages were disintegrating and wood carving had seriously declined. Nevertheless, totem-pole carving continued until 1900 in most parts of the area. After 1900, the art actually increased in a few Kwakiutl and Tsimshian villages and spread to villages where poles had not previously been made. Mask making has also survived in some villages.

PLATE I

a. Bryan Peel, the Nass River carver, using the drill. Note the tool box and two unfinished rattles
b. Using the straight knife on the upper half of a rattle. The lower half lies on the work block
c. Using the adz to shape the lower half of a rattle

(Photos by V. E. Garfield, 1934)

PLATE II

b

a

c

d

a. Tsimshian Mask (*Provincial Museum, 1517. Victoria*)
b. Haida Mask (*Provincial Museum, 1506. Victoria*)
c. Tsimshian, Headdress Mask (Tlingit type) (*Museum of the American Indian, Heye Foundation 9/8031*)
d. Kwakiutl Mask (*Provincial Museum, 2314. Victoria*)

PLATE III

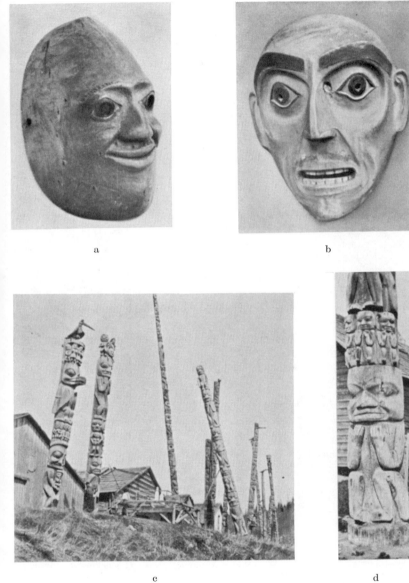

a   b

c   d

a. Tsimshian Mask (Nisqa) (*Museum of the American Indian, Heye Foundation, 6/676*)
b. Tsimshian Mask (*Portland Art Museum 48.3.398*)
c. Tsimshian Totem Poles, Kitskan Village of Kilwaukool, B. C. (*Photo by G. T. Emmons, 1909, courtesy American Museum of Natural History*)
d. Detail, Tsimshian Totem Pole, Kitskan Village, Hazelton, B. C. (*Photo by G. T. Emmons, 1909, courtes American Museum of Natural History*)

PLATE IV

a

b

c

a. Tlingit Totem Pole, along Main Street, Wrangel, Alaska (*Photo courtesy American Museum of Natural History*)

b. Haida Totem Pole, Skidgate Village, B.C. (*Photo courtesy Museum of the American Indian, Heye Foundation*)

c. Kwakiutl Totem Pole, Zeballus, B.C. (*Photo courtes British Columbia Travel Bureau, Victoria*)

Plate V

a. Tsimshian Wooden Hat (Tlingit type) (*Museum of the American Indian, Heye Foundation, 2/9165*)

b. Tsimshian Rattle (*Portland Art Museum, (48.3.366)*)

c. Chilkat Blanket (Tlingit) (*Denver Art Museum, RC-5-P*)

PLATE VI

a   b

a. Mask and costume impersonating "Small-slave-of-the-Tlingit," worn by John Sarahnitz
   of Kitwanga, Skeena River
b. Guxsan, of Gitsegyuhla on the Skeena, singing a gambler's invocation

(Photos by M. Barbeau, 1924)

PLATE VII

b

a

a. Manoesk, head chief of the Eagle clans of the upper Nass River, wearing ceremonial costume *(Photo by M. Barbeau, 1927 or 1929)*

b. Hagwelgyet performers of a secret society ritual at the canyon of the Bulkley River near Hazelton *(Photo by Barbeau, 1920)*

PART 2

PAUL S.WINGERT

TSIMSHIAN SCULPTURE

CHAPTER SEVEN

TSIMSHIAN SCULPTURE

A distinguishing feature in the culture of a people is its art style. It is possible by the analysis of an art to discern two groups of elements that combine to form a style. These groups may be called the general and the specific. The general elements appear in the recurrent use of certain shapes, proportions, lines, and colors, and in the rhythmic accented relationships and the symmetrical dispositions that result from the manner in which they are customarily arranged. The specific elements include the treatment of surfaces and the conception and rendering of detail. It is necessary for an understanding of an art style to consider the role played by both of these groups of elements.

Careful and thoughtful observation is essential for the characterization of any art style. This is especially true for the art of the Tsimshian and, indeed, for the polychromed wood sculpture of all of the northern Northwest Coast. Even a casual familiarity with this art reveals that Tsimshian, Haida, Tlingit, and northern Kwakiutl sculpture share many general and even specific elements of style.[1] The shared elements in this art are, in fact, so numerous that one can distinguish a basic or common art tradition for this part of the Northwest Coast. And yet a close study of the sculpture discloses important differences that make it possible to identify tribal styles. The determination of these tribal styles depends, however, upon the recognition of the differences that are typical of the art of the various tribes. These differences are, in the majority of cases, the consequences of an emphasis or of a particular development that is given to certain of the commonly shared style elements. It is, therefore, important to consider in any study of Northwest Coast art the style elements that are shared throughout the area before characterizing a tribal style. Tsimshian art will, consequently, be examined after the common denominators of Northwest Coast art as a whole have been determined.

Although a number of important studies have been made of this art,[2] there has been no attempt to single out tribal styles. Yet it is obvious that even a tentative designation of tribal styles by means of comparative

---

[1] The Bella Coola, since they are not direct neighbors of the Tsimshian, will not be included in this study.

[2] Boas, 1927; Emmons, 1930; Davis, 1949; Inverarity, 1950; etc. See also Garfield in this volume, pp. 58—63, 67—70.

analytical methods will add considerably to our knowledge. Typical examples of the art of the area as a whole must be selected from the art of the various tribal groups and subjected to analysis in order to determine the broad common denominators of style. It will then be possible with this as a background to discover, by examining a larger representative group of tribal examples, the elements distinctive of tribal style.

The present study must be considered a preliminary or pioneering attempt in this direction. It aims to present: (1) the problems involved in any study of the art styles of the Northwest Coast area as a whole or of any particular tribal group; and (2) a method of handling the complex matter of stylistic analysis and characterization. A good deal of intensive work will be required to document examples of the art of the various tribal groups before the present preliminary study can be expanded. But it would appear that the methodology set forth in this study may profitably be used and developed in any further research in Northwest Coast style considerations.

Northwest Coast Art

The sculpture of northern coastal British Columbia, the islands off the coast including the Queen Charlottes, and southeastern Alaska, consists of a number of like objects. These include masks, so-called "totem" poles, house posts, rattles, horn spoons, boxes, and headdresses (Pls. 2—5).[3] Wood, particularly red cedar, was the preferred material, although horn, bone, and ivory were often used. Shell, fur, and shredded cedar bark were frequently added as decorative materials. Adzes of various sizes were the commonly employed carving tools. The sculptures were with rare exceptions polychromed, the colors most generally applied being reds, yellows, blue, a bluegreen, black, and white. These were mixed with fish-egg oils and the painting may, therefore, be considered a variant of a tempera technique. The paint was applied directly to the wood without any base and the resulting effect was that of a flat mat color.

Life forms served as basic subject matter for the art of the entire area. Human, animal, bird, and fish forms appear singly or in various combinations. Even in the purely and semi-fantastic shapes it is apparent that subject matter was largely derived from experiences with life forms, since the imaginative elements are usually supplementary to them. It should be noted that this fauna is a naturalistic one with which all of the tribes were familiar. The content or meaning of this common subject matter was, on the other hand, extraordinarily variable. Similar human, animal, bird, or fish forms may, for example, have entirely different

---

[3] Unless otherwise indicated credit for photographs is due the museum possessing the object.

connotations within the mythology of the various tribal groups. But the use of similar life forms is typical of the art of the entire area.

These life forms are rendered in a number of commonly found expressive ways. This representation may in many instances be termed realistic, since it describes life forms with considerable accuracy (Pl. 2,a). Distortion, simplification, and bisection are, in other examples, adaptations of this realism in order to apply the form to a particular surface or shape. An example of what may be called adaptative realism appears on the painted or the low-relief carved and painted house fronts.[4] The animal form usually represented here depicts over the doorway the head of the animal seen frontally, while to left and right are delineations in profile of the two halves of the figure that result from a longitudinal bisection. A comparable adaptation is also frequently found on totem poles (Pl. 4, b). The desire to present the most distinguishing features of a form often leads to the use of non-realistic conventionalization which is derived from and stands for the intended form. In some instances, such as on masks, rattles, boxes, and blankets, this conventionalization is carried so far, or such a small portion of it is used, that the effect is close to a geometric abstraction (Pl. 5, c). Since these conventions are a method of indicating in a precise way the most recognizable features of a form, they may properly be considered symbols. Whether a form is represented realistically, or is adapted to fit a space or a surface, or is depicted by one or more conventional shapes or designs, the concept usually embraces the total form. This is often shown on carved and/or painted masks.

Dispersion of these methods of representation throughout the area is one of the unique features of the art. Excellence of technique is also characteristic of this sculpture. Three techniques are employed in the realization of subject matter: the shapes and details of many subjects are rendered sculpturally, either in three-dimensions or in varying degrees of high or low relief; linear designs follow a surface function in the same way; or these linear and sculptural techniques are combined in the same work. Color is extensively applied to emphasize, or further describe, the separate parts or details of a carving.

Masks

The common or shared elements of Northwest Coast art, as well as the peculiar tribal style characteristics, appear most clearly in masks and totem-pole carvings, which are the two types of sculpture with both the widest distribution and the closest relationships to individual tribal ideas. Masks representing human features, often sensitively rendered,

[4] Cf. Inverarity, 1950, Pl. 2.

are more frequently found among the Tlingit and the Tsimshian, while those with animal, animal and human, or fantastic features are found throughout the area (Pls. 2—3). All Northwest Coast masks consist of carved forms with an incised line definition of details and an extensive use of polychromy. The basic aesthetic principles evident in these carvings are remarkably consistent and indicate conclusively that a single tradition dominated the art of the entire area. But tribal styles can be recognized on the basis of preferred design elements, a sensitivity to certain forms, and the rendering of specific details.

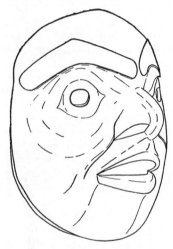

Figure 4. Kwakiutl Mask.

The shape commonly stressed in these masks is a wide geometric ovoid (Fig. 4).[5] It is usually emphasized by and contained within a sculpturally expressed outline which is sometimes broken by projecting parts, such as ears. The surfaces have a prominent lateral curvature and frequently a less emphatic vertical curvature of similar kind. Carved planes, lines, and shapes define in the majority of examples expressive facial forms and give a depth and projection to these features. Although a totality of shape is always clearly presented, there is, however, an important difference in the degree of emphasis on the mass or volume of facial forms. Many Haida and Kwakiutl masks, for example, have heavy, bulky forms that stress the weightiness and mass of the carvings (Pl. 2, b, d); while some of the most typical Tlingit and Tsimshian masks express the inner cubic content of the forms as they press against and expand the surface (Pls. 2, a; 3, b). There is, therefore, either an expression of mass and heaviness or of volume and lightness. This is in either case revealed sculpturally. Painted forms and areas are constantly used to further this expression.[6]

The carved forms of the majority of Northwest Coast masks are fragmented into many separate and marked off parts (Pl. 2, d). Some of these, such as brows, eyes, nose, and mouth, are strongly defined sculpturally and are further emphasized by the application of a flat paint (Fig. 5). Other parts, especially the symbolic designs, are often merely painted on the surface, although they are also sometimes designated by

[5] Figures numbered 4—18 in this text were drawn by Robert M. Watts.
[6] See also Wingert, 1949 b.

finely incised outlines. This emphatic division of form and surface must be considered characteristic. But, whether carved or painted, the forms and surfaces tend to stress and to follow the outline of the mask. When the mask is observed frontally, however, the painted designs and the painted carved forms produce in many examples an appearance of flattened surfaces which conceal from this point of view the sculptural character of the forms. To see them successfully it is necessary to have at least a three-quarter frontal view of the mask. The over-all effect of the division of the form and surfaces into a number of separate shapes is to increase the apparent size of the mask, since these parts are bold in scale and establish a strong unity of expression.

The use of line, both aesthetically and expressively, is of great importance in all of the art forms of the Northwest Coast. This is particularly evident in the masks. Two types of line may be discerned (Fig. 5). The one, a "resultant line" is the consequence of the meeting of two planes of different angles or depth, which are frequently painted in contrasting colors (Pl. 2, c, d). The other is a "pure line," either a painted or incised delineation on or into the surface. It is less common than resultant line and is sometimes used with the latter to represent further a shape or an area, or to separate, define, or describe areas or forms. The line is, in every case, emphatic, clear, and precise. It is a fundamental and a strongly apparent feature of this art.

Figure 5. Kwakiutl Mask Design.

The quality of line varies from thin or fine to a moderate heaviness, although it is, in every instance, remarkably regular and controlled. A long line, smoothly modulated to the surface planes predominates with few exceptions, while the short, staccato line is rarely used. Curved lines, sometimes changing direction abruptly and dramatically, as in the resultant lines of the eyebrows, are a striking feature of this style (Fig. 5). Although the lines generally follow in a subtle manner the surface planes, there is a strong tendency for both the resultant and the pure lines either to connect or to be closely associated, thereby forming an over-all pattern distinct from that of the carved forms. A conflict or tension is thus produced between the lines and the sculptured forms which contributes dramatically to the expressive power of the masks.

Color is used extensively as an adjunct to line (Pl. 2 d). Delineated or carved surface patterns, whether used symbolically or descriptively, are usually painted in a flat color tone contrasting with that of the surrounding areas. Incised lines are frequently filled in with a color of different tone or intensity from that of the detail or form delineated by them. Pure line is also often painted on the surface in a conspicuously contrasting color. While preferences vary somewhat from tribe to tribe, red, yellow, black, and white are the most commonly used colors.

A number of design elements and principles are also shared in the masks. The design is generally composed of several clearly separated and distinct parts which are large in scale and give the mask an appearance of size incommensurate with its actual size. A bilateral vertical division, either tangibly represented or strongly implied by the prominent vertical axis of the nose, creates in most instances an absolute symmetry. Significantly related to this axis is the large inverted triangle defined by the longitudinal eyebrow line, as its base, and the sharply tapering chin, as its apex (Fig. 6). The downward movement of this heavy triangle is more than counteracted by the vigorous upward thrust of another triangle with its apex at the bridge of the nose and its base along the vertical of the mouth. There results an interlocking arrangement of triangles that both focuses and equilibrates attention on the eyes and the mouth. The sweep of the eyebrows, the emphasized chin, and the sculptured mouth make this interlocking geometric pattern clear (Pl. 3, b).

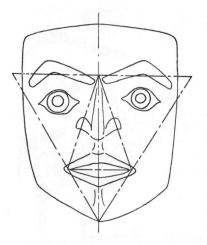

Figure 6. Diagram, mask design.

An essential feature of mask design is the way the component lines by their directional character integrate the internal or surface design elements with the exterior outline. Both resultant and pure lines are often repeated and convey rhythmic relationships. Many of these lines may be characterized as angular curves (Fig. 7). An important aspect of Northwest Coast mask design is the frequent use of angular curves of similar kind as reverse motives, a factor contributing considerably to the unity of aesthetic expression. An effective unity is also achieved by the interaction of design elements of similar shape or size. The sculptured and painted forms and areas are as a result brought into a significant visual and expressive relationship.

Although the surface designs follow the carved forms, it is important to note that they have a distinct identity. When seen frontally many of the masks have, for example, by virtue of their surface designs, a flat, two-dimensional appearance.[7] But, when they are seen laterally, the true depth and prominence of the carved forms are very apparent. It is therefore evident that a tension exists between the surface designs and the sculptured forms (Fig. 7). This is true even though the design elements usually follow the structural forms of the surfaces. The design is, in every instance, closely integrated.

There are, also, aside from the general elements, certain shared specific or subtle style features. These, too, are of extreme importance for an understanding of this art. The handling of surfaces, for example, embodies a textural quality of particular sculptural and expressive importance. This ranges from smooth surfaces to those where adz marks impart a plastic depth and variety (Pls. 2, a; 3, a). Painted lines or areas also contribute to the variety of surface effects. The larger carved planes and forms together with the delineation of smaller areas combine to create a rich and significant composite that is particularly indicative of this sculpture (Fig. 7). Surface forms, rendered in a smooth or in a modelled textural manner, may express either the quality of bulk or mass, or that of interior content or

Figure 7. Tsimshian Mask.

volume. Bulk or mass is described by the strength of statement of projecting or recessive forms; while volume is indicated by a tight, thin, smooth surface treatment (Pl. 2, a, d). The fact that surfaces are often representative or descriptive is usually supplementary to their basic expressive and aesthetic qualities.

Perhaps no other feature of Northwest Coast sculpture is so widely shared and is so important for an understanding of the art as the rendering of details. The characterization of tribal styles depends heavily on the recognition of preferences for certain details and their use to emphasize structural and expressive parts. This is particularly evident in masks.

Regardless of tribal provenience, details are in the majority of instances clear, precise, and ample in scale. They stress especially the vigor

[7] Cf. Inverarity, 1950, Pls. 69, 71.

and integrated character of the design. This is evident, for example, in the crisp carving of the sweeping curves of the eyebrows, in the sharp elongated line that often marks the bridge of the nose, and in the deeply cut semi-circular line of the nostrils (Fig. 8). Depressed lines or areas, frequently carved flanking the mouth, contribute considerably to the expression of animation. But, particularly conspicuous are those details used customarily in rendering the eye. The outline of the eye is usually an oval flanked by two sharp points (Fig. 5). It is represented either by a fine low relief line or by an equally fine painted outline. The concept of the eye shape is in some cases integrated with a depressed surrounding area in which the eye is delineated by a sharp, clean line caused by the meeting of the plane of the surrounding area with the lines of the eye itself (Pl. 3, b). The pupil, usually large, circular, and pierced, is often outlined by a painted or by a carved relief line. Although varying greatly from example to example, the mouth is usually emphasized by protruding, sculpturally described lips. Painted surface details are another constant style feature of masks. They are used independently to delineate symbols, to function in a decorative manner, and to define further the carved details. These painted details are rendered in commonly shared color combinations, although variations in tone and in intensity often indicate tribal preferences (Pl. 2, c, d).

Figure 8. Tsimshian Mask.

An analysis of Northwest Coast masks reveals that they are the product of a widespread art tradition with many elements shared by all of the tribal groups. The greater number of these elements are general, basic style characteristics and make it possible to identify readily a mask from this area. It is important to realize, however, that certain of these basic features are in many instances developed further and become marked tribal style features.

Totem Poles

One of the most widely known and typical art forms of the Northwest Coast is the carved pole, which occurs in various sizes and kinds. These poles show in their style numerous common denominators comparable to those discovered in the masks. But, certain peculiarities in the elements of this art denote tribal differences. Frequently referred to as "totem" poles, they include monumental memorial and grave poles and interior and exterior house posts, usually of structural function. With rare exceptions, the "poles" are only half or three-quarter round, the back of them being cut off as a flat surface or hollowed out by the removal of the heartwood. The basic shape is, therefore, a segment of a solid or hollow vertical column, the rounded surface of which provides a field for sculptural forms. The curvature of this surface is, to a large extent, analagous to that of the masks.

A number of fundamental style elements, regardless of tribal provenience, are held in common by this Northwest Coast art. The carved forms are, with few exceptions, so adapted to the surface that the original geometric shape of the log is retained (Pl. 3, c). But the dramatic contrast of projecting and recessed shapes imparts to the pole an expansiveness and an expressed diameter far greater than its measurable one. Verticality and height are also emphasized. The concept of presenting subject matter by superimposing a number of figures or shapes visually dramatizes verticality; while the varied sizes of the carved figures and the comparatively slow visual ascent, occasioned by areas that attract and hold the eye for a moment, contribute appreciably to the expression of height. In many examples, the over-all shape of a pole consists of separate and closely marked off parts which are inter-related in a number of ways to produce a unity of effect. Mass, bulk, and weight are constantly evident in the carved forms on these poles, but the expression of an inner volume expanding or pressing against the surface is also a common style element. A potential or expressive movement is likewise typical. It is frequently conveyed by tense, dramatic poses or by the relationships between figures, and it is often intensified by the expanding volume of the forms.

Practically the full range of sculptural techniques appear in varying degrees on Northwest Coast poles. Forms carved in the round, however, are not common, especially in the north. Low and high relief carving and incised lines were used throughout the area. With the exception of one type of Tlingit pole, a conspicuously basic feature of this sculpture was the utilization of the full curve of the front surface for the carving and delineation of the larger heads of the principal human and animal figures represented. These heads have, therefore, a maximum of available roundness which expresses that of the original pole. Arms and legs and other details are frequently carved in high relief on the surface.

A great number of Northwest Coast totem poles reveal the origin of their design in linear prototypes. This is evident in the extensive use of planes to create the illusion of depth and roundness and in the major role played in all totem-pole designs by varieties of linear effects. The use of planes and lines may, in fact, be considered basic to totem-pole style. Planes either follow the original curvature of the pole or, more commonly, are cut into the surface at almost every possible angle to it (Pl. 4, b). This use of planes dramatically defines and separates parts and gives to the carving a visual variety and an expression of depth far greater than that which actually exists. There is often combined with these planes a sharp, deep, and oblique undercutting which furthers the illusion of depth, mass, and volume. It is also a device used to transform or to adapt a flat linear design to fit a partially three-dimensional surface.

Line is of extraordinary importance in this art. The kinds of line used vary from extremely thin or delicate to very heavy or deep. Although a linear effect is typical, the line is often not a pure but is a resultant one (Pl. 4, b). Both forms and details are rendered by this type of line and there is produced, as a consequence, a sharp linear division of surface. Pure line, often deeply incised, is also at times used to delineate details, such as eyebrows, ears, nostrils, and teeth. In either case, the line has a sweep and a breadth of movement which agrees with and accentuates the dynamic character of the carving. Light washes of color are used within the line delineations to represent or reveal further a shape or detail. Color also serves to define or to separate the major from the minor parts of a form. The expansive movement and the important relationships between lines is well illustrated by the often monumental curve of the eyebrows, a curve sensitively shaped which carries the eye of the observer to and from the outline of the head and is frequently related to a like or reverse curve in the lower part of the facial design.

Totem-pole designs show rather striking differences. These differences are often indicative of tribal style peculiarities, although many general design elements are shared throughout the area. The columnar shape of the pole and the nature of the subject matter it was intended to convey are basic to the design of totem-pole sculpture. The fundamental problem in this art was the vertical arrangement of a number of human and animal and semi-human and semi-animal forms to represent with proper emphasis clan crests, incidents relative to them, and other narrative subject matter. The challenge to the designer was to achieve the requisite effects within the difficult field provided by the half-cylindrical surface of the pole.

Three principal types of over-all design were used: (1) the superposition of figures arranged in clearly marked off horizontal zones which follow the curvature of the surface — this appears to have been the classic and preferred Tsimshian type (Fig. 9); (2) the organization of superposed forms in an interlocking system along the vertical axis of the pole, utilizing and often deeply cutting into the surface — this is a typical Haida type (Pl. 4, b); and (3) the superposition of separated horizontal shapes which are developed from all sides within the mass of the pole, the original surface counting for little in the final appearance — this type is found most commonly among the Tlingit (Pl. 4, a). Various combinations of these types occur in many instances. Numerous Haida poles, for example, combine design principles of Types 1 and 2, while some southern Tlingit poles are only slightly modified versions of Type 1. Many examples of Kwakiutl poles produce a unique effect by combining Types 1 and 3 (Pl. 4, c). In a number of examples, however, many design elements are shared in common.

A frequent stylistic feature of totem-pole design is the sculptural expansion of the major shapes which are, in turn, separated one from the other (Pl. 3, c). Within these major divisions there is further segmentation of details. The major and minor forms are both usually represented by deep relief carving in which a varied angling of planes in respect to the surface plane is of conspicuous importance. Other parts are divided by incised surface lines and by painted areas. The importance in the design of separated areas is evident in every case.

Figure 9.
Tsimshian
Totem Pole.

Figure 10.
Haida Totem
Pole.

An exaggeration in the rendering of heads, whether human, animal, or composite, is fundamental to pole design (Fig. 10). In practically every example these are arranged in a vertical, rhythmical pattern. This is a repetitious pattern often broken by smaller design elements. Within the over-all design these repetitious elements are often alternating and are composed of a number of varied shapes. Rhythmic relationships are usually vertically oriented and are seldom obvious. The heavily accented parts are of extreme importance in these designs. While they practically always carry the balanced and rhythmical elements, they also function in the design because of their sculptural prominence. The rendering of these distinctive parts often places a totem pole within a broad traditional area and sometimes within specific tribal limits.

The rhythmic handling of design elements, so fundamental to Northwest Coast pole sculpture, is supplemented by several other equally important features. The concept of the relative size of the figures represented and of the system of proportions followed in the rendering of each figure is of particular significance. Figures of strikingly contrasting sizes not only impart an aesthetic richness to the design by their variety, but also give a dramatic expression of scale and monumentality, since the small figures serve as a unit of measurement (Pl. 3, d). It is evident that this scale is independent of the actual size of the pole, for it appears comparably in the small wooden and argelite models. The tendency to use a like set of proportions for both the large and the small figures carved on the same pole is also of the utmost importance in the expression of monumentality. This is particularly characteristic of the classic type of Tsimshian pole.

A unity of over-all effect is, in the majority of instances, less typical than a unified relationship that is established between the accented major parts. The presence of such relationships is common to totem-pole design, but the varied methods employed to achieve these results appear to denote individual tribal style elements.

The specific style features shared in totem-pole sculpture are evident in the rendering of surfaces and in the preference for details of a particular character. A textural quality is often given to the surface. This is achieved by an adzing which varies greatly from a very fine technique resulting in an almost smooth finish to a coarser treatment with the adz marks actually producing an uneven geometrical pattern (Pl. 3, d). The boldness and variety of surface planes is the consequence of a desire to depict every form and every detail with the utmost clarity. Paint is used to denote further the role played by each plane and detail within the design. Variations in depth, angle, and texture of surface planes also contribute greatly to the visual expression of movement which draws the eye vertically up and down the pole. Since these planes are skillfully carved to utilize different effects of outdoor light, their full importance is somewhat diminished when a totem pole is seen within a museum.

The emphasis placed upon certain details is another common denominator of totem-pole style, although the precise rendering of that detail may be considered of tribal significance. Human, animal, and bird heads are usually, as previously mentioned, enlarged and sculpturally emphasized in many different ways. Within the expansive shape of the head the eyes and the mouth are often conspicuously exaggerated (Fig. 11). The wide sweep of the brow above the eyes frequently serves as a plane which dramatically combines the expressive force of the eyes, while the heavy sculptural form of the nose functions similarly in association with the mouth. Totem-pole detail is rendered in a clean, precise, and emphatic technique. The detail is usually large in scale and is often so simplified that it may be considered symbolic rather than descriptive of subject matter. Although the greater proportion of detail is carved in a strong, well-controlled line or in an emphatic high or low relief, a fair amount is also painted on the carved and delineated shapes.

An analysis of the style of Northwest Coast totem poles discloses, just as that of the masks, the presence of a considerable number of general style elements. These are shared in common to such an extent that a broad dominating tradition must be recognized for the art of this entire region. Further evidence in support of this conclusion appears in the widespread occurrence of many specific and, at times, identical style features. But, in the art of the totem pole and, although perhaps less certainly, in that of the mask, the preference for and the greater development of certain general and specific style elements, in combination with what may be considered a few local style peculiarities, clearly indicate the existence of tribal styles within this basic tradition.

Common Style Elements

To recapitulate: a great number of common style elements, both general and specific, are basic to the art of the mask and the totem pole (Pls. 2—4). These are shared by the Tsimshian with their neighbors the Haida, the Tlingit, and the Kwakiutl. The carving of masks and poles follows and expresses in every case the original shape of the materials from which they were carved. The horizontal curvature of the section of the log, which pro-   Figure 11.
vides the surface for the sculpture, is, for example,   Tsimshian
always expressed in the fully carved forms. There is   Totem Pole.
also an equally strong emphasis in both masks and poles on the verticality of the original shape of the material. The over-all shape is divided into a number of conspicuously separated and articulated parts. A largeness of scale, measurable by the contrast of small and large elements used in expressing form, gives to the masks and to the poles a quality of monumentality. Both types of sculpture emphasize depth and projection of carved planes, lines, and shapes. It appears that, although tribal styles are suggested by an individual interpretation of general style features, these over-all style elements remain constant and fixed. Of particular significance, for example, is the way in which the outline is stressed and is kept within compositional limits. There is, in the art of this entire area, a remarkably rich and varied vocabulary of expressive sculptural forms.

Line, both resultant and pure, is a striking feature of this sculpture. It is extraordinarily regular and controlled, and it is clean and precise in character. Although it is always strong in quality, it varies from thin to heavy. A long, smoothly modulated line is characteristic, but this line often defines a slow moving angular curve. Its prime function is to represent and to separate the major and minor shapes and parts. These parts are further described by color, which is also sometimes used to emphasize both types of line. An expressed or implied movement is, moreover, frequently conveyed by a line which moves over the surface independently of the sculptured shapes. All lines follow the surface planes and tend to connect the form with an over-all pattern.

The principles of design common to mask and totem pole are closely based on the maximum utilization of the original shape of the material. Designs are, therefore, organized both horizontally and vertically. But there is either a stated or suggested bilateral, vertical division that frequently results in an absolute symmetry. This vertical division often furnishes the main axis of the design. While this axis is the focal point in mask design, it usually shares that role in totem poles with a number of horizontal crossing axes. A further basic difference in mask and totem pole design is the expression of movement conveyed by the relationships between elements. In masks, for example, a strongly marked lateral movement prevails, but in totem-pole design the stressed movement is vertical, a movement enriched by pauses provided by minor horizontal excursions. The various design elements are rendered, in both art forms, as separate parts, set off sculpturally and by color, and usually delineated by a resultant or by a pure line. There exists between these separated parts a subtle rhythmic interrelationship which is often the result of repetition or of inversion of entire, or fragments of similar, design elements. The total effect is one of an interesting, interlocked design unity combined with a rich and varied aesthetic expression. The scale and monumentality observed in the proportioning of design elements furthers this dramatic appearance.

The treatment of surfaces is of particular importance in Northwest Coast art. In both mask and totem-pole carvings they are given a varied textural quality. This ranges from those examples in which the adz marks are prominent to those in which the surface is completely smooth. An expansive quality exists in the majority of surfaces and contributes appreciably, as though a consequence of an inner pressure, to a textural expression. The bold handling of planes, frequently placed at sharp angles to each other, together with a sculptural projection and recession of parts, give to the surfaces remarkable contrasts in depth and form. This adds greatly to a textural expression. Color is also used to give added variety to surface textures. The treatment of surfaces, therefore, not only produces a strong visual response, but it also arouses a marked tactile reaction in the spectator.

Specific shared elements appear conspicuously in certain general characteristics of detail. All detail is clear and precise in definition and ample in scale. Color is used constantly either to pick out carved details or to render, independently, surface details. Especially typical of the detail on masks and totem poles is the exaggeration of facial features, such as eyes, mouths, eyebrows, and noses. These enlarged features impart an even greater appearance of size to the already large heads. Detail is, in general, a simplified description of actuality; but here it is, at times, developed to such an extent that it functions as a symbol. The character of the detail usually stresses the vigor and integrated nature of the design.

Tribal Styles

Tsimshian art can only be considered as representing a tribal style when the unique features which distinguish it from the elements shared by the art of the entire area are singled out and brought together. This is also true for the characterization of any other Northwest Coast tribal style. In the case of Tsimshian and other tribal arts of the Coast it must be recognized that, while distinctive styles can be discovered, a good deal of the art may be considered marginal and will evidence, therefore,

style elements typical of the art of neighboring groups. It is important to note that many of the tribal style elements are also elements common to the art of the area and have been given a particular emphasis or treatment. These elements must be considered, in consequence of this special treatment, manifestations of tribal style.

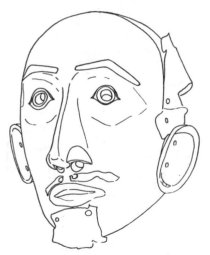

Figure 12. Tsimshian Mask.

Tsimshian. The distinctive features of Tsimshian art appear most clearly in their masks and totem poles. The over-all design of Tsimshian masks emphasizes the enclosing outline of the original shape of the material (Pls. 2, a; 3, b, c). This is usually a sharp line, a line which prevails whether or not there are projections, such as ears. The original shape of the mask as a segment of a columnar form is stressed in the final shape. Tsimshian style is especially evident in masks with human features (Fig. 12). The designs of these masks are built firmly upon the interlocked reverse triangles of eyebrow to chin and of mouth to bridge of nose (Fig. 6). The visual foci are, therefore, equally distributed between mouth and eyes. In the majority of examples, the eyes and mouth are very carefully and clearly carved and are scaled nearly to human proportions.

These masks often evidence a remarkable expression of naturalistic bony structure and fleshy form. The orbital, jaw, and cheek bones are, for example, usually rendered with marked sensitivity. There is also a strong expression of fleshy forms and tightly drawn surface skin over these bony structures. The bulk and heaviness of individual parts and of the total form is, therefore, often less emphasized than the bony structure of the head and the skin membrane covering it (Pl. 3, b). The result is an expression of comparative lightness and of inner cubic content of form.

Tsimshian masks of this distinctive human type usually represent a maximum use of resultant, and a minimum use of pure, line. The entire design is, in fact, rendered in sculptural terms: that is, all of the features and structural forms are portrayed in varying degrees of relief. This relief, whether the outlining of an eye, the definition of eyebrows, or the taut handling of surfaces over bony structural members, is substantially a sensitive sculptural style.

Surface treatment is also indicative in these masks of a tribal style. Surfaces tend to be smoothly rendered and show a marked sensitivity of structure and form. This is accomplished sculpturally and depends relatively little upon line or color definition. Planes defining surfaces are often carved with considerable subtlety and variety. They range in size from the large continuous one that represents the forehead to the many small ones that combine to describe the eye area and the cheeks. Sur-

Figure 13. Tsimshian Mask.

faces are, in general, more naturalistic and less dramatically stylized than is characteristic of other Northwest Coast mask styles.

In expression, too, Tsimshian masks of this type depend upon the elements of naturalism (Fig. 13). These are handled with directness and restraint, and there is little dependence on excessive distortion or elaboration of detail. This is even true of the most dramatically expressive masks. The rendering of form is, in a number of instances, so personalized that there can be little doubt that the mask is a portrait (Pls. 2, a; 3, c).

Tsimshian totem poles demonstrate even more emphatically the presence of a tribal style. The type of pole characterized as "classic Tsimshian"[8] is best representative of the distinctive elements of this style (Pl. 3, a). Important among these elements are the basic conception of a carved pole, the organization of the design, the principles of rhythm and balance, the sense of scale, the system of proportions, and the sculptural technique employed. The concept of the pole as a vertical shaft with a curving surface is strongly expressed. The arrangement of the figures in a series of clearly defined superimposed horizontal divisions confirms visually the convex curvature of the surface, while the rhythmic repetition of figures or parts of figures, often in an alternating system and usually with variety, carries the eye upward and stresses verticality and height (Fig. 14). Scale is further conveyed by the use of two sizes of figures of practically the same proportions, one very small, the other very large (Pl. 3, d). Both figures and descriptive details are considerably simplified and stand in closer relationship to life forms than is usually the case in Northwest Coast totem-pole representations. The figures, whether human, animal, or bird, are rendered in a strongly sculptural technique expressive of three-dimensional form. Detail is not elaborated but is usually rendered in varied low relief carving rather than by the use of surface lines. Important details and major expressive elements in the design, especially those which carried the rhythmic pattern, were further emphasized by color.[9]

Figure 14.
Tsimshian
Totem Pole.

Figure 15.
Detail,
Tsimshian
Totem Pole.

[8] Cf. Fig. 9, above.

[9] Color was used sparingly and only in this way on the older poles. A more extensive use of brighter colors dates later when commercial pigments were combined with or supplanted those of native manufacture.

The expressive character of Tsimshian totem-pole sculpture is one of clarity, sobriety, and restraint. Crests, legends, and narratives are depicted by comparatively few figures, rather than as in other totem-pole styles by dramatic exaggeration of statement in form and detail. Tsimshian expression depends upon what can be called "measured pauses." These result from the horizontal separation of the superimposed forms and the tendency to separate the larger forms by interspersing zones of smaller figures (Fig. 15; Pl. 3, d). The smaller figures produce a visual pause and give a lucidity to the presentation of subjects. The eye is carried, because of this design, in a rather slow methodical manner from zone to zone. The visual interest is, however, richly rewarded by subtle variations and interrelationships between forms.

Haida. The "classic Tsimshian" type of totem pole appears in other areas, although it receives its greatest development among the Tsimshian. Totem poles of typical Haida style, in contrast, utilize the entire surface as a continuous field for decoration (Pl. 4, b; Fig. 10). Strongly accented forms, it is true, are clearly presented as superimposed and are sculpturally separated, suggesting horizontal divisions. But a varied array of supplementary forms overlap and interlock the larger elements and give to the design the visual effect of a continuous development along a vertical axis. Dramatic presentation of subject matter is also characteristic of Haida style. The subjects most commonly represented are animal, fish, and bird forms, usually with spectacular exaggerations of the life forms on which they were based. Human figures, usually small in size, often appear as minor elements in the design. The multiplicity of detail and the frequently complex interrelationships create the impression of verbosity in the depiction of crests, legends, and narratives, as compared with the economy and lucidity of statement by the Tsimshian. An important difference is also apparent in basic sculptural concepts. Haida forms, unlike those of classic Tsimshian style, develop in depth and therefore utilize the bulk of the pole more completely than its surface.

Tlingit. Tlingit totem poles of typical style are, in many respects, closer to the classic Tsimshian type than to Haida (Fig. 16). Tlingit poles are often of slighter diameter than those of either the Tsimshian or Haida and represent a series of separated superimposed forms. The concept is, however, not so much that of a carved pole as that of a number of independently conceived sculptures arranged in a vertical sequence (Pl. 3, a). Tlingit technique, in contrast to the Tsimshian method of carving forms with the surface and to the Haida habit of cutting

Figure 16.
Tlingit
Totem Pole.

deeply into the surface, develops independently of the original convex curvature of the pole. Their forms are carved from the sides as well as from the front and have, therefore, often the appearance of fully round sculptures. The extensive use of attached projecting parts further the expression of a free spatial setting of the forms. Also characteristic of Tlingit style is the often comparatively smaller scale of parts, the elaborateness of detail, and a more extensive use of color. Poles of this distinguishing type frequently lack the sculptural dignity of statement of the Tsimshian, or the baroque-like complexity and power of the Haida poles.

Kwakiutl. Kwakiutl totem poles are largely eclectic in style. Typical designs consist of two or more large scale figures, separated horizontally from each other, and vertically superimposed (Fig. 17). Bird and animal forms, or the bodies of human figures, have, in many cases, the strongly sculptured simplified naturalism that distinguishes Kwakiutl carvings in the round (Pl. 4, c); in other instances they seem derived from Haida or Tsimshian pro-

Figure 17. Kwakiutl Totem Pole.

totypes. But typically Kwakiutl is the tendency to carve the large heads of human, bird, animal, or mythological beings as though they were masks and to give them the dramatic intensity of sculptural expression so characteric of Kwakiutl masks (Fig. 18). The full development of Kwakiutl totem poles, especially in southern British Columbia and Vancouver Island, evidences a marked degree of skillful virtuosity.

Linear and Sculptural Styles

A broad summarization of Tsimshian and other northern tribal styles can be made on the basis of masks and totem poles. It is necessary first to recognize in the art of this area two basic styles: the one, a linear-surface style, and the other, a sculptural-volume-depth style. Neither one is mutually exclusive of the other, although there is often greater emphasis in tribal styles on one or the other. The preference for representing subject matter must also be considered before any broad generalizations can be made. These preferences fall into three groups: (1) a realism in which the visual representation of natural forms is stressed; (2) an adaptative-realism in which natural forms are modified in order to accomodate them to a shape or surface; and (3) a conventionalized-symbolism in which the most identifying parts or details of a subject are reduced to a design to stand for the entire subject. Any summarization of tribal styles must take into account these two basic styles and the preferences for representing subject matter. In Tsimshian masks and totem poles, a sculptural rather than a linear style is dominant. This sculptural expression is simplified, or reduced to essentials, and conveys matter whenever possible in a realistic way or in a slightly adaptive-realistic manner. Linear treatment and a conventionalized-symbolism are seldom found in this art. The sculptural handling is controlled in technique and moderate in expression.

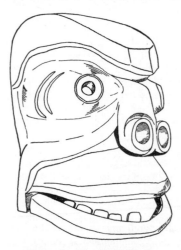

Figure 18. Kwakiutl Mask.

In contrast to Tsimshian sculpture that of the Haida emphasizes almost in equal measure both the sculptural and the linear styles. The treatment of subject-matter tends more towards an adaptive-realism than that of the Tsimshian. In certain instances, strongly sculptured and simplified realistic figures appear; and in other examples, conventionalized-symbolism is resorted to. The sculptural character of Haida style is, however, often powerful. Tlingit art stresses a linear overlay of realistically carved forms. Line is customarily used to emphasize small scale details. These details are usually rendered in a conventionalized-symbolic manner and detract from the basic realism of the forms. The result is frequently an art of weak statement and one in which the full expression of the carved forms is at times vitiated by linear patterns. Kwakiutl art relies upon often spectacularly sculptured forms, although it, too, utilizes the possibilities of linear-surface design (Fig. 18). Realistic and adaptive-realistic forms therefore dominate; but a conventionalized-symbolic expression is sometimes resorted to. Kwakiutl art is consequently the most varied of Northwest Coast styles.

Tsimshian sculpture can be considered, in art history terminology, "classical;" Haida, "classical to baroque;" Tlingit, largely "rococo;" and Kwakiutl, a vigorous "eclecticism." In every instance, however, examples can be found that will deny such broad generalizations. But such examples merely seem to document the fact that all Northwest Coast styles have a number of elements in common. Tsimshian art, in comparison with that of the surrounding tribal groups, manifests an austerity, clarity, and precision that marks it off from other Northwest Coast styles.

Tsimshian Sculpture

Although a characterization of Tsimshian art is more dependent on masks and totem poles than on any other category of their sculpture, it seems necessary, nevertheless, to consider to what extent these style characteristics appear in other objects. The raven or chief's rattle is perhaps the most developed of these sculptures (Pls. 1; 5, b). It is posssible that this type of rattle was of Tsimshian origin, but by the time of extensive European contact it was common to all of the northern Northwest Coast tribes. These rattles are examples of the most technically complex sculptures of the area. The basic forms are simple structural parts rendered in three dimensions, while the delicate shaping of these parts and of the detail that enriches their meaning are of extreme refinement, and yet vigorous in statement. Color is used extensively to accent forms and details. Documented Tsimshian examples excell in design and technique, and tend to substantiate the tradition that this type of carving originated among them. These rattles are substantially realistic in style — that is, they describe reality in a visual sense. It is important to note that they are both conceived and carved in a strongly three-dimensional manner. Solid forms and negative space are emphasized and both contribute effectively to the final result.

Other sculptured objects of the Northwest Coast include hats or helmets (Pl. 5, a), horn spoons, and boxes or containers (Fig. 2 and details of Pl. 1). With the exception of woven blankets (Pl. 5, c), there seem to be no clear-cut tribal styles associated with any of these objects. The carved forms and painted details are common to the art of the entire area. The conclusion that may be drawn is that these forms were disseminated before European contact and, being old, manifest a conglomeration of style elements. They must, therefore, be evaluated as examples of general and not of specific Northwest Coast styles.

Characteristic of this art as a whole is the stress placed on sculptured forms and detail rather then on painted surface designs. As indicated above, this is distinctive of masks and totem poles and it is also typical of all other carved objects. Although Northwest Coast art is preeminently a polychromed sculpture, color is always of secondary importance to that of sculptured shapes. But the extensive use of color serves the important purpose of further describing the significant parts of the sculptured forms.

Tsimshian art may be said to embody two sets of interdependent style features: those which are common to the art of the entire northern part of the Northwest Coast, and those which reveal tribal traits, the latter, in many instances, merely consisting of an emphasis on or a development of various common style features. These two major stylistic groups are not, however, distinctive components of Tsimshian style alone, but appear in every tribal style of the area.

It is possible on the basis of this study to characterize and to evaluate Tsimshian art. It is an art of restraint and of simplified clarity in both its style features and its expressive intentions. There is less over-statement of content or over-elaboration of detail than in any other tribal art of the northern Northwest Coast area. The lucidity of form development and the economy of rendering detail are typical of this art. In a region where sculpture is the important means of aesthetic expression, Tsimshian art represents a particularly high accomplishment. This is approached most nearly, although with a greater elaboration of detail, by the art of the Haida. Tsimshian sculpture must be considered the "classic" style of the Northwest Coast, if the term "classic" is used to designate clarity of definition, simplicity and directness of interpretation, and restraint in expression.

Any evaluation of Tsimshian sculpture must stress these stylistic features. The art is particularly rewarding in its strong aesthetic qualities. These require discerning observation and reveal, as a consequence, rich visual effects. But, typical of the art of the entire area, these results also produce a strong tacticle response. Sculpture and painting often collaborate. Color emphasizes the carved forms and details and in many instances adds to them. Moreover, it gives an effect that contributes substantially to the initial visual response to the forms. That initial response is, after renewed contacts, often supplanted by one stimulated by the merging of sculptural and expressive forms. It is necessary to examine any object of Tsimshian art many times before a true comprehension of its forms, and an appreciation of its aesthetic qualities, can be arrived at. The resulting knowledge and pleasure are, however, more than worth the effort. Tsimshian sculpture is certainly one of the great arts of the Northwest Coast and is just as certainly one of the significant art expressions of the American Indian.

BIBLIOGRAPHY

ARCTANDER, JOHN W.
  1909. *The Apostles of Alaska.* New York.

BARBBEAU, MARIUS
  1917. "Growth and Federation in the Tsimshian Phratries." Proceedings of
         the 19th International Congress of Americanists. Washington.
  1929. *Totem Poles of the Gitksan, Upper Skeena River, British Columbia.*
         Canada Department of Mines, Bulletin 1, Anthropological Series,
         No. 12. Ottawa.

BARNETT, H. G.
  1938. "The Nature of the Potlatch." *American Anthropologist,* Vol. 40,
         No. 3.
  1942. "The Southern Extent of Totem Pole Carving." *Pacific Northwest
         Qarterly,* Vol .33.

BENEDICT, RUTH F.
  1923. *The Concept of the Guardian Spirit in North America.* Memoirs of the
         American Anthropological Association, No. 29.

BIRKET-SMITH, KAJ, and FREDERICA DE LAGUNA
  1938. *The Eyak Indians of the Copper River Delta, Alaska.* Copenhagen.

BOAS, FRANZ
  1895. "Report on the North-western Tribes of Canada." *Tenth Report of
         the British Association for the Advancement of Science.*
  1897a. "The Social Organization and Secret Societies of the Kwakiutl
         Indians." *Report of the U.S. National Museum.*
  1897b. "Decorative Art of the Indians of the North Pacific Coast." *American
         Museum of Natural History, Bulletin* 9.
  1902. *Tsimshian Texts.* Bureau of American Ethnology, Bulletin 27.
         Washington.
  1916. *Tsimshian Mythology.* Bureau of American Ethnology, Annual
         Report 31. Washington.
  1927. *Primitive Art.* Oslo.
  1930. *Tsimshian.* Handbook of American Indian Languages, Bureau of
         American Ethnology, Bulletin 40. Washington.

CODERE, HELEN
  1950. *Fighting with Property: A Study of Kwakiutl Potlatching and Warfare,
         1792—1930.* Monographs of the American Ethnological Society,
         No. 18.

DAVIDSON, D. S.
  1937. *Snowshoes.* Memoirs of the American Philosophical Society, Vol. 6.

DAVIS, ROBERT T.
  1949. *Native Arts of the Pacific Northwest.* Stanford.

BIBLIOGRAPHY

DEE, HENRY D., Ed.
1944—45. *The Journal of John Work, 1835.* British Columbia Historical Quarterly, Vols. 8 and 9. Victoria.

DRUCKER, PHILIP
1939. "Rank, Wealth and Kinship in Northwest Coast Society." *American Anthropologist,* Vol. 41, No. 1.
1948. "The Antiquity of the Northwest Totem Pole." *Journal of the Washington Academy of Sciences,* Vol. 38, No. 12.

EMMONS, G. T.
1903. *The Chilkat Blanket.* American Museum of Natural History, Bulletin 3.
1925. "The Kitikshan and Their Totem Poles." *Natural History,* Vol. 25, No. 1.
1930. "The Art of the Northwest Coast." *Natural History,* Vol. 30.

GARFIELD, VIOLA E.
1939. *Tsimshian Clan and Society.* University of Washington, Publications in Anthropology, Vol. 7, No. 3.

GARFIELD, VIOLA E., and LINN A. FORREST
1949. *The Wolf and the Raven.* Seattle.

GOLDSCHMIDT, WALTER R., and THEODORE H. HAAS
1946. "Possessory Rights of the Natives of Southeastern Alaska." Office of Indian Affairs. Chicago. (Mimeographed)

GRENFELL, CAPT. HAROLD R. N., Trans.
1938. "The Journal of Jacinto Caaman." *British Columbia Historical Quarterly,* Vol. 2

HAEBERLIN, H. K.
1918. "Principles of Aesthetic Form in the Art of the North Pacific Coast." *American Anthropologist,* Vol. 20, pp. 258—264.

HATT, GUDMUND
1949. *Asiatic Influences in American Folklore.* Det Kgl. Danske Videnshabernes Selskab Historik-Filologiske Meddeleser, Bind 31, Nr. 6. Copenhagen.

HERZOG, GEORGE
1949. "Salish Music." In *Indians of the Urban Northwest,* ed. M. W. Smith, pp. 93—110. New York.

HOIJER, HARRY, and others
1946. *Linguistic Structures of Native America.* Viking Fund Publication in Anthropology, No. 6

INVERARITY, R. B.
1950. *Art of the Northwest Coast Indians.* Berkeley.

JOCHELSON, WALDEMAR
1905. *Religion and Myths of the Koryak.* Jessup North Pacific Expedition, Vol. 6.
1924. *The Yukaghir and the Yukaghirized Tungus.* Jessup North Pacific Expedition, Vol. 9.

KEITHAHN, E. L.
   1945. *Monuments in Cedar.* Ketchikan, Alaska.

KINDAITI, KYOSUKE
   1941. *Ainu Life and Legends.* Tokyo.

KRIEGER, HERBERT W.
   1927. *Indian Villages of Southeast Alaska.* Smithsonian Institution, Annual
      Report. •

LEVI-STRAUSS, C.
   1943. "Art of the Northwest Coast at the American Museum of Natural
      History." *Gazette des Beaux Arts,* Vol. 24, pp. 175—183.

MACLEOD, W. C.
   1928. "Economic Aspects of Indigenous American Slavery." *American
      Anthropologist,* Vol. 30.

MCILWRAITH, T. F.
   1948. *The Bella Coola Indians.* 2 Vols. Toronto.

MURDOCK, G. P.
   1934. "Kinship and Social Behavior among the Haida." *American Anthro-
      pologist,* Vol. 36.
   1936. *Rank and Potlatch among the Haida.* Yale University Publications
      in Anthropology, Vol. 13.

NELSON, E. W.
   1899. *The Eskimo about Bering Strait.* Bureau of American Ethnology,
      Annual Report, No. 18, Washington.

NEWCOMBE, W. A.
   1931. *British Columbia Totem Poles.* Report of the Provincial Museum of
      Natural History for the year 1930. Victoria.

NIBLACK, ALBERT P.
   1890. *The Coast Indians of Southern Alaska and Northern British Columbia.*
      Report of the U.S. National Museum.

OLSON, RONALD L.
   1927. "Clan and Moiety in Native America." *University of California
      Publications in American Archaeology and Ethnology.* Berkeley.

PAALEN, WOLFGANG
   1943. "Totem Art." *Dyn,* No. 4—5. Mexico.

QUIMBY, GEORGE I.
   1948. "Culture Contact on the Northwest Coast, 1785—1795." *American
      Anthropologist,* Vol. 50.

RANDALL, BETTY U.
   1949. "The Cinderella Theme in Northwest Coast Folklore." In *Indians of
      the Urban Northwest,* ed. M. W. Smith, pp. 243—286. New York.

RICKARD, T. A.
   1939. "The Use of Iron and Copper by the Indians of British Columbia."
      British Columbia Historical Quarterly, Vol. 3.

SAPIR, EDWARD
   1915. "*A Sketch of the Social Organization of the Nass River Indians.* Canada
      Department of Mines, Museum Bulletin, No. 19. Ottawa.

SHOTRIDGE, L.
  1919. "A Visit to the Tsimshian Indians." *Museum Journal*, Museum of the University of Pennsylvania, Vol. 10, pp. 49—67; 117—148.

SWANTON, JOHN R.
  1905. *Haida Texts and Myths.* Bureau of American Ethnology, Bulletin 29. Washington.
  1909. *Tlingit Myths and Texts.* Bureau of American Ethnology, Bulletin 39. Washington.

SWANTON, JOHN R., and FRANZ BOAS
  1912. *Haida Songs. Tsimshian Texts.* Publications of the American Ethnological Society, Vol. 3.

THOMPSON, STITH
  1929. *Tales of the North American Indians.* Cambridge.

WINGERT, PAUL S.
  1949a. *American Indian Sculpture: A Study of the Northwest Coast.* New York.
  1949b. "Coast Salish Painting." In *Indians of the Urban Northwest.* ed. M. W. Smith, pp. 77—92. New York.